FEELINGS FIRST
SHADOW
WORK

A SIMPLE APPROACH TO SELF LOVE AND EMOTIONAL MASTERY (WITH JOURNAL PROMPTS)

BY
BENJY SHERER

DISCLAIMER

I am not, nor have I ever claimed to be, a medical professional of any sorts. The statements and methods in this book have not been evaluated by any governing board.

I believe, however, and have seen in my clients that the statements made in this book are all intuitively obvious... once they are said. They make immediate sense to a mind that is ready to receive them. The tools, wisdom and methods in this book are derived from a lifetime's worth of introspection and analysis into the human condition and from my own personal experience and research.

My academic background is in Philosophy and World Religions. I have spent a lifetime searching for answers through various lenses, and - after an awakening of my own - I learned and pieced together the comprehensive guide to self-love that you are about to learn.

I recommend that you read this book with an attitude of "take what resonates and leave what doesn't". This book will absolutely give you a whole new perspective on your life, your emotions, and your subconscious cycles that have been keeping you stuck, but my goal is not to 'convince' you of anything, it is merely to shine light on what you have never managed to see for yourself.

"The unexamined life is not worth living."

—SOCRATES—

"... and the unlived life is not worth examining."

—ME—

ACKNOWLEDGMENTS

To my Dad, who gave me every last bit of love he knew how to give. I am truly grateful for all the support you have given me along the way. Thank you for the freedom with which you allowed and encouraged me to live my life.

To my Mom, who rarely knew what to say to me but was always there to listen. I realize now that you have always been my best friend. Thank you for all the love you have given me. I hope to continue making you proud as I help to change lives with this work.

To my Twin Flame, the strange love I felt for you broke my reality so that I could learn everything that I am now teaching to people. You are the one person without whom none of this would be possible. I will always cherish the good times and I hope this book helps you find your way as well.

ABOUT THE AUTHOR

There is a fine line between emotional awareness and spiritual awakening, and that is where Benjy thrives as a mentor and teacher. Guiding people to emotional mastery, Benjy bridges the gaps between spirituality, psychology and philosophy. Those 3 realms are all intrinsically connected in Benjy's completely unique - and yet intuitively and compellingly simple - approach to self-love and emotional mastery.

Growing up with a deep existential need for answers, Benjy's academic background was in Philosophy and World Religions, but that academic search left him pessimistic at the soul level about our ultimate role in this universe and the purpose of life. It wasn't until after a dark night of the soul and a spiritual awakening of his own that he was forced to dive more deeply into his own inner healing, in order to rediscover his true purpose and learn the skills, tools, and techniques that he teaches to clients today.

His overall approach is about "Feelings First", referring to the notion that we can master our emotions directly, without the need for deep intellectual analysis, ultra-spiritual practices, or pharmaceutical medications. He teaches people how to connect directly with the emotions and sensations of their body - without fear, guilt or shame - and to allow these feelings to run through them so that they can be truly released. It's about building emotional muscle, not seeking rational answers.

As he says, emotional healing is NOT an intellectual activity.

CONTENTS

INTRODUCTION

Hello and welcome to your easy-to-understand guide to shadow work, inner healing and emotional mastery! I am truly thrilled and honored to have you here and I am genuinely excited that more people are choosing to start doing this inner work every day. The world is reaching a tipping point of awakened people and it's beautiful.

With every person that chooses to go on this journey - to heal their wounds and become a better and more loving version of themselves - we collectively take a little step forward. Bit by bit, this is quite literally how we change the world. No joke. One by one we change ourselves, and as we change ourselves, we change the way that we treat others and - through our changed behavior - we lead others toward their own awakenings and changes. Over time, we all move forward and the whole world evolves.

Thank you for being on this journey with us. Thank you for being here with me in this book. Thank you for having the strength and courage to dive into your triggers and negative programming to finally heal and release them. Thank you for having the courage to take on fear and to learn to connect to your emotions again.

The fear of feeling our uncomfortable emotions and unresolved trauma is at the very core of everything that has gone wrong on this Earth over thousands of years. A common phrase that floats around the spiritual and emotional healing communities is, 'hurt people, hurt people'. In other words, people who are in pain cause pain to others. This is a fundamental truth of humanity that we all need to recognize and accept in order to help us move into the next stage of our evolution. If you could begin to understand that everyone who is being cruel to you is actually in a lot of pain themselves and that this pain has been passed down from generation to generation for millennia, you'd be able to start being a little less defensive and judgmental and we could all start opening ourselves up again.

The cycles of pain and trauma that we're experiencing today started so long ago that most people can't even fathom how deeply these cycles are embedded into human society. By bottling up the pain that we don't know how to deal with in moments of trauma we develop defense mechanisms that protect us, but that also keep us going in circles, continually projecting our pain onto the outside world and causing more pain and trauma to ourselves and others, thereby perpetuating this cycle over and over.

If we don't heal these things within ourselves in time, then we pass them down to our children through our behavior, and even through genetic memory. Only now are enough people starting to 'wake up' and free themselves from these trauma loops that the Earth is ready to make a real shift forward.

Here's the main secret that more people need to discover so that we can collectively evolve to the next stage of humanity:

In order to be truly at peace and happy we need to fully love ourselves, and people who love themselves are kind to others, because being unkind to others causes us pain - even when we don't realize it. We are naturally empathic at our cores. The more connected we are to our own emotions, the more connected we are to the emotions of others.

So, someone who is truly connected to their own emotions and who fully loves themselves would never knowingly cause harm to another, because they would feel that pain themselves and/or be aware of the self-harm involved in harming someone else. They are aware of the stain that this leaves on their souls.

When you knowingly cause someone pain, you shoot neurons down certain pathways in your brain and create certain emotional frequencies within yourself that - their existence inside of you - programs your own brain for fear and anger and other corrosive and harmful emotions that reinforce negative behavior patterns.

When we cause pain to someone else, we cause ourselves pain as well. When we ignore someone else's pain, we are also ignoring our own pain. Most of us are just too disconnected from our own emotions to notice. We've done such a great job of putting up walls around our pain that we can't recognize that it's there. Finally reconnecting to our emotions is what the collective awakening is all about. Bit by bit, we are reincorporating lost parts of ourselves that we shut down to help us survive, so that we can remember who we truly are and start moving towards a brighter future.

Welcome to that journey. The world, the universe and all of humanity thanks you.

This book is meant to give you the full foundation of knowledge that you'll need to start your healing in a safe, efficient, and healthy way, without getting trapped in the darkness of your past trauma while you do. First, we are going to learn about shadow work, about our emotional cycles, and about the foundational concept of self-love. Then we are going to learn the full 8 step process that I use with my clients to get through a lifetime's worth of healing in record time.

Lastly, at the end of this book we are going to embark on a 21-day journaling challenge with reflection exercises to help guide you through the first stage of your healing; to help teach you how to connect to your emotions again and learn to bypass your conscious mind to get right to your heart.

PLEASE do not get started on the journal exercises before reading this whole book. The journal prompts - without all the overarching wisdom I'm going to give you in this book - won't be truly effective because you will still be approaching the journaling from the same mind and perspective that you have done everything else in your life, which will thereby defeat the entire purpose of you trying to learn how to finally react to things differently. We need to change the entire way that you approach your emotional healing in the first place, before we can really make any progress.

This book is about making a complete shift in your perspective about your life, your emotions, and your inner healing so that you can be READY to make the changes we want to make, using tools like journaling.

It's not about the journaling... it's about the energy, attitude, and intention you bring to your journaling. When you understand that, you will understand how inner healing can be happening at each and every moment of your life without chasing down your trauma and inner demons. You will learn how to turn every single moment of emotional distress into a moment of healing, learning, and growth by flipping your understanding of what these moments of distress are really all about.

Sounds good?

Awesome. Let's do this!

WHY DO SHADOW WORK?

Ok... so... before we really get into anything else, let's do a quick "what is shadow work and why am I bothering to do this?"

I'll be explaining Shadow Work in more depth as we go, but for now - to put it as simply as possible - I would say that it is the process of learning how to reconnect with our emotions by breaking the barriers we have put up against our pain. It is the method of learning how to finally observe, confront, heal and release all the unresolved emotional trauma inside of us so that we can live in a more heart centered way. It is the collection of tools, techniques, and intellectual wisdom that we need to keep with us, practice and maintain so that we can live a life free from fear, fully expressing our true selves, and engaging in healthy, mutually beneficial relationships with everything and everyone around us.

You will come to understand more and more through this book and through your journey that everyone on this planet is in a lot of pain... and none of them know how to deal with it, so they project that pain outwards onto others, taking out their unresolved issues on the people closest to them without realizing it, and thereby perpetuating trauma cycles over and over.

You will come to understand that there are no truly cruel and hateful people in the world... only wounded and tortured souls. You will see how those who act the worst are actually in the most pain - though they generally don't recognize it. They are so disconnected from their emotions that emotional pain doesn't truly register to them. They are numbed out. They are asleep. They are living in a hazy fog of auto-pilot, fear-based defense mechanisms. Their souls have been beaten into submission by the outside world.

> *It all has to do with states of consciousness and levels of self-awareness.*

As humanity moved forward in evolution, it wasn't the physical changes to our bodies that were most important in distinguishing our species as unique. Perspective. Insight. Thought. Self-awareness. These are the things that gave us the unique characteristics it took to push us from Neanderthals to our modern selves. We gained enough awareness to investigate ourselves and the universe in new ways. We advanced science, we made inventions, we came to understand our place in the universe a little better, etc... This is how we got to where we are.

But now... it's time to evolve again.

How aware and conscious are you REALLY???

Have you been noticing how your emotions have been controlling your life? Have you noticed all the little ways that you are getting triggered each and every day into being defensive, judgmental, angry, frustrated, and a whole slew of other uncomfortable, unpleasant, and unhelpful emotions that make you act in ways that don't actually serve your best interests and that you generally regret later on? Do you recognize the shame cycles that this puts you into and how shame exacerbates the problem? Do you recognize how those triggers that sparked this negative cycle to begin with were never really about the thing that triggered you at all, but actually just about deep-seated insecurities in yourself that you never dealt with?

Do you notice and observe all the ways that you act in response to these things that trigger you, and how it is actually your response to these situations that is making your life worse most of the time... NOT the actual thing that happened that triggered you? Do you notice the role that you are playing in perpetuating all the cycles that keep you from progressing in your life? Do you notice that the things that you are running from inside of you couldn't actually hurt you if you were to stop running from them, and that you running from them is actually what's causing all of your problems?

Do you recognize how causing someone else pain actually leaves a stain on your subconscious mind that creates subconscious distress that you then need to spend your lifetime bottling up, justifying and rationalizing, and how this cycle leads to you hurting yourself and hurting others even more, thereby reinforcing this cycle, over and over and over and over?

Have you been truly aware of the relationship between your head, your heart, and your gut? Do you TRULY know who you are, and understand the forces driving your decision making?

Have you been observing that YOU... and fear... are at the center of all of your suffering, and that you have had the ability to take control of this cycle the whole time?

Probably not.

Even if you're thinking 'yes' right now... Ehhhh... probably not. It goes deeper than you probably think or are ready to realize just yet. Your subconscious programming goes so deep that you have only glimpsed the tip of the iceberg. The more that you come to understand how everything is energy and how the brain programs itself in response to unresolved emotions, the more you'll realize how you've actually been running on auto-pilot your whole life. Your entire life has just been programmed responses to trauma that you never dealt with, but it's time to wake up, Neo.

If you haven't truly come to see and understand all the little cycles that drive you to make your decisions, then how conscious and aware have you truly been? You've been asleep in your own body your whole life, letting unconscious emotional cycles guide all of your decisions while you deluded yourself into thinking that you were actually in charge and acting according to strict rationality and logic the whole time.

Recognizing these cycles and becoming more self-aware so that we can take conscious control over our lives and not let unresolved emotions rule our behavior is the next necessary stage of the collective evolution of our species. We need to recognize these subconscious patterns and bring them to the surface so that we can end these self-harming cycles before we destroy ourselves.

You will come to see this era of your life and of humanity (before our awakening and healing) in the same way that you look at the middle ages... We were such fools to do so much harm to ourselves and others in such brutal and barbaric ways.

But... we just didn't know any better! And that's the point. Neither do you. Not yet. You've never been taught a better way to deal with all the emotions that are trapped inside of you that are at the root of all of your suffering.

This is why we do shadow work. To uncover the core of who you are again and to help you rediscover all the lost parts of yourself that you left behind somewhere in the past because people made you feel bad about yourself for having them. To be able to learn to live in alignment with who we are at our cores instead of putting on a mask and pretending to be someone we're not. To be able to live with inner peace and a true sense of self-actualization. To put aside fear of judgment and criticism, and to be unapologetically ourselves in the face of dissent. To stand up for love - for ourselves and others - in all situations. To evolve ourselves to a higher state of self-awareness so that we can attain the next stage of what human intellect is capable of - when it is not restricted by the self-harming patterns and limiting beliefs of our emotional defense mechanisms.

We do shadow work to be able to overcome the primitive cycles of our pseudo self-aware selves that we have been in for millennia. We do it to overcome the need to resort to judgment and anger, and to instead find the strength and courage and inner knowing to treat anyone who mistreats us with compassion - both for our benefit and theirs, because the very concepts of anger and judgment just don't feel good anymore.

We do shadow work to finally and fully escape the self-perpetuating emotional pain cycles that we've been in our whole lives. Anxiety, overwhelm, stress, fear, doubt, guilt, shame, jealousy, etc... All of these are actually just your emotional body's way of telling you that something is wrong... and you never learned to listen! Shadow work will teach you how to listen, so that those uncomfortable emotions can finally lead you back to the true you.

Shadow work is the key to your new life.

Or... for those that resonate with the following terminology - it is your ticket to 5D.

It is all that you need to do in order to find your true path, purpose, and bliss on this earth.

Don't take that the wrong way. That doesn't mean that as soon as you complete some level of your inner healing a genie comes down and grants you all the things you've been waiting for in your life. No... it doesn't work that way... no matter how much you believe in manifesting and law of attraction. Instead, by doing the shadow work you will learn to enjoy and appreciate exactly where you are 1,000 times more while you continue to do the work towards a better future, and this gratitude, ease and inner peace will help you take better actions, and notice and follow opportunities that you wouldn't have before, creating an upwards cycle in your life where things just start getting better and better.

The more that you master yourself and your emotions, the more immune you are to life's little challenges, and so the better you handle them and the more success you see. Inner improvement perpetuates itself in this way. The more that you raise your inner frequency, the more that you stay calm and confident and take actions that will improve your life. The more that you improve your life, the more that you raise your inner frequency, leading you to take better actions, etc...

See how that works? Improving your inner world helps you naturally improve your outer world, which in turn improves your inner world, and around and around we go.

Here's the thing though... the opposite of that is true as well and THAT is where you have been living.

Because of your fear, trauma and limiting beliefs you have been living in a negative spiral where you would make decisions from fear which then in turn had negative consequences on your life, which then made you feel a certain way, which then made you act a certain way, which then had certain consequences, etc... Do you see the cycle that's going on here? Emotions lead to actions. Actions lead to consequences. Those consequences create more emotions and around and around and around we go.

Most people have been trying to solve this problematic cycle in a backwards way. Most people try to end this cycle by changing their actions, thinking that if they change their actions that it will change their external worlds, and that will change how they feel so that they can start acting in an even better way. Basically, they try to solve their external problems first, hoping that when their lives get better externally, they will feel better internally and the cycle will change.

Well... let me ask you... how has that been working out for you so far? Has chasing external gratification helped you master your emotions, or do you find yourself constantly chasing something that seems just out of reach?

What I am proposing is that you change your approach to breaking this cycle and choose a different starting point.

Change your emotions! Learn to master your emotions FIRST! Make THAT your primary goal in every moment of your life. That is the only way to truly end this cycle because no amount of external change is going to be able to truly change how you feel. You know... money can't buy happiness and love. Success and safety in the external world will never make you feel successful and secure if you don't already feel that way inside, but feeling that way inside FIRST will lead you to make choices that will get you there externally. You've spent your life trying to solve things the wrong way around. You've focused on the outer world (which you can't control), as opposed to your inner world (that you actually have more direct access to and can control). When you change just one element of this cycle, the whole pattern changes... so let's start by changing the one element that we have the MOST control over, then watch our lives change as a result of that.

Like I said.... You haven't yet realized the full depth of how you have been betraying and sabotaging yourself all this time because you were not yet at a state of consciousness where you could observe the subconscious emotional cycles that were keeping you trapped. EVERY SINGLE AREA of your life has been dominated by your unconscious programming that you developed as defense mechanisms against trauma.

If you want to know why we do shadow work, I'll let one of my clients tell you herself. Kristy had been struggling with depression and suicidal tendencies for 10+ years before finding me, and after being in my course for only 8 weeks she posted the following in my Facebook group:

"Here's what I accomplished after having an awakening and doing some conscious shadow work:

1. Freedom from my past
2. Waking up happy
3. A sense of well-being
4. A stronger connection with my higher self
5. A better relationship with my partner

I sound like a walking infomercial!" (Kristy D).

So, if you want to learn the safest and easiest methods to dive into your shadow and claim back the true you that you left behind a long time ago; to start living without fear, guilt, or shame about who you are so that you can evolve into your best self and live the life you were actually meant to live on this planet, then read on. I am going to show you how simple it can be. It's not usually easy... but it IS simple, and it doesn't have to take half as long or be half as painful as you think it does.

We will dive into a whole bunch of explanations, exercises and crucial nuggets of paradigm altering wisdom, and then we will get to the 21-day journaling journey, but FIRST...

DISCLAIMER!

The big disclaimer that I need to give you is this; even though I am going to give you a series of journal prompts to help you start your healing, I do NOT believe journaling to be a supremely effective way of doing shadow work or of really and truly healing your wounds! No amount of journaling is going to get you over your issues.

3 obvious questions then come to mind...

1. Why isn't journaling effective?
2. What IS the most effective way of healing?
3. Why on Earth are you giving me journal prompts if it's NOT going to help?!?!?!"

Allow me to deal with that last question first.

Why will we use journaling?

Firstly, despite believing that journaling is not supremely effective, I didn't say that it is NOT AT ALL effective... It's not that it can't help at all. It's just that - in my opinion - it's a 'level 1' version of doing your shadow work. It can only deal with the most superficial levels of our healing when done in the way that most people do it. It can only truly get you so far. Nonetheless, journaling is still helpful for beginners to get started and I know that many of you are searching for shadow work journals, so I'm happy to oblige.

I'm giving you this disclaimer not to dissuade you from doing any journaling, but rather to make sure that you temper your expectations about what journaling alone can do and to prepare you for the need to go deeper. It is unlikely that you will see the kinds of massive changes in your life through journaling that true shadow work can do for you.

Improved self-esteem, improved relationships, increased confidence, elimination of anxiety, overcoming depression and suicidal thoughts, leaving toxic relationships, improved relationship with money, increased career motivation, increased courage and confidence, and SO SO MUCH more.... These are all things that clients of mine have experienced by doing the real shadow work with me and reconnecting to their emotions. You will likely see some progress in these areas by journaling if you do it properly, but really, you'll just be skimming the surface of what's possible.

The second reason I'm giving this disclaimer is so that I can help you understand how to best use journaling to get more out of it than you would have otherwise. Once you understand why journaling is not usually effective, you'll be able to use journaling in a way that actually can be more effective.

HOW we use the method is of more consequence than the logistics of the method itself. So, understanding the limitations will help you avoid falling into those traps. We are going to use journaling as a way to help you reconnect with your emotions and to start building the muscles that you will use when you do the real inner healing. We will use it to prepare you for what comes next.

Why is journaling NOT effective?

Not only do I believe that journaling is ineffective, but I believe it can actually stall your progress on this inner healing journey because it promotes a grand misconception about inner healing that will keep you going in circles forever. Namely, the misconception that shadow work and inner healing is ultimately an intellectual activity.

Shadow work is NOT an intellectual activity!

It is an EMOTIONAL one!

The real problem that you are trying to solve in your life is NOT in the past. It's NOT your memories. It's NOT the traumas that you experienced. None of those things matter right now. None of those are why you are suffering in the present moment. Yes... your cycles of suffering originated in those past traumatic moments, but the past is gone. It's not why you're suffering now.

The REAL problem that you are dealing with is merely the unresolved emotional energy that is still trapped inside of you. The emotions that never had an opportunity to be expressed and released during a moment of trauma. It is these emotions that you still carry right now, not the past events that caused them, that are at the core of your suffering. Our mission isn't to focus on what caused your suffering in the past, but rather to focus on what's causing your suffering right now. From there, we can slowly work our way down to the more deeply buried unresolved emotions naturally.

Let me try and express it like this...

Imagine that when you were 6 years old you were taught that sweating is impolite or maybe even dangerous. Imagine that you were made to believe that sweating would lead you to be judged, mocked, rejected, or hurt. As a result of this belief, you did everything you could not to sweat, and let's just say that you managed to train yourself not to sweat... ever.

So, every time your body started heating up, instead of releasing sweat through the pores of your skin like it needed to in order to stay healthy and function properly, this sweat got rerouted, trapped and stored inside of you. Every ounce of sweat that needed to get released got stored up inside of you instead, and you started building up this reservoir of unreleased sweat inside of yourself, storing it wherever you could find space and cluttering up your organs and blood stream with this stored up, toxic sweat. There were moments when this normal, natural bodily function of sweating needed to happen, but you prevented it from happening, holding the sweat inside instead.

Well... this is what we have been doing with our emotions our whole life.

When we experienced undesirable or uncomfortable emotions that we weren't safe to - and didn't know how to - deal with in the moment, we stuffed them down. We chose not to express and release them because doing so in the moment would have led to more pain and trauma. We learned over our lifetimes that crying was undesirable, that expressing ourselves would have us judged or mocked, that being vulnerable would lead to rejection and abandonment, and therefore we trained ourselves NOT to cry, NOT to express ourselves, NOT to be vulnerable... and so much more.

We developed all kinds of defense mechanisms to keep us from having to feel our emotions in the moment and to help us avoid running into similar scenarios that would bring up the same emotion in the future. We trained ourselves not to release any of that sweat that was coming up inside of us, and we trained ourselves to avoid doing anything that might lead us to having to sweat in the future.

Thing is though... if you were actually to work out and not sweat... YOU... WOULD... DIE!

Literally. You would basically boil alive from the inside out.

There's actually a medical condition called Anhidrosis (the inability to sweat) and it is often fatal because the body can't cool itself. Sufferers of anhidrosis often die from heat stroke.

Well, the same has been happening with your emotional body. You've been keeping this stuff inside for so long that your emotional body has been slowly rotting away from the inside out. The brain shut down your connection to your heart as a defense mechanism to help you avoid feeling the uncomfortable emotions that you didn't know how to deal with, and you've held this stuff in for so long that your body has actually reprogrammed itself to be completely unable to release them. It's like your body has forgotten how to sweat. Your brain shut down that function and has semi-permanently rerouted all sweating functions to another part of your body. The connection between your sweat glands and your pores has been shut off and reprogrammed.

Your brain did this because it thought it was protecting you, and in the moment... it was (because you actually weren't safe in that moment of initial trauma to express and release those emotions), but we never realized before how this was affecting us in the long term. We kept on telling our emotional bodies "store this away, and I'll deal with it later when I'm safe", but we never came back to deal with it later. So, we completely forgot where our pain was coming from, and we never realized how our past pain is still affecting us today.

Think back to - say - the 50's... where the concept that "well... my dad beat me as a child so MAYBE that has an effect on my self-esteem and how I treat people" was all kinds of new age psycho-babble poppycock! The real manly men of that era didn't want to hear all this nonsense about emotions and women weren't given any input on the matter at all. Emotions made you weak. Our whole society was built on emotional repression in countless ways. This is why toxic masculinity runs rampant, by the way.

All this stuff about trauma cycles and abuse that just seems so painfully obvious to us about basic human psychology now was news back then... and it was questionable news at that! It was still a 'theory' that maybe being traumatized as a kid affected your development and personality as an adult. Geez... Dark times.

But I digress...

The point of bringing up this metaphor of sweating was to help express that in order to heal now, we do NOT need to think about every push up, every sit up, every mile you ever ran, etc... We don't need to focus on the things that should have made you sweat in the first place. We are NOT AT ALL concerned with those past events specifically or directly. They are irrelevant to the pain your body is in at this moment.

Instead, we are ONLY concerned with the fact that there is a reservoir of harmful, toxic sweat inside of you that needs to be released. We need to get rid of this toxic stuff, and logic and rationality about what created that toxicity to begin has nothing to do with it. We only need to learn how to reconnect your pores to this pool of trapped sweat inside of you so that we can FINALLY start letting it go, and when we are free and clear of all that old sweat inside of us, we can fill up that space (that used to be filled with this toxic sludge), with clean and healthy cells that will make us stronger, happier and healthier.

In other words, our goal is not to focus on the past, but only to release that which we still carry within us right now, and the easiest way to do that is by focusing on what we are experiencing RIGHT NOW! Your present emotions are connecting you to your past subconsciously, so you don't need to analyze it further. You only need to allow your emotions to guide you.

THAT is the goal of *Feelings First Shadow Work*. To learn how to reconnect our conscious minds and our experience of ourselves and our worlds with our emotional bodies that we have spent a lifetime running from. It is actually about BYPASSING the brain and connecting to the heart and to our emotions directly, allowing unresolved emotions to release themselves naturally. We are trying to reconnect our sweat glands to our pores so that all the stuff that we never expressed can finally be dealt with. We can slowly start draining that pool of trapped sweat that we've been carrying with us our whole lives.

As we do this, any revelations or memories that we need will come up on their own, but that will be a natural byproduct of doing the emotional healing. It is not our primary goal. Your subconscious brain is already fully aware of all these intellectual revelations that you think you need to know, and as you learn to relax and stop resisting your emotions, your brain will be able to open up to these insights and revelations. You will become aware of them consciously in a natural way when you stop running from the emotions that are connected to them. You don't need to seek them out. You don't need 'answers'. You only need relief.

The great news here is that - contrary to popular belief - in order for you to overcome your past traumas, triggers and fears, you do NOT need to spend your days focusing on those traumas and fears! This healing journey can be SO MUCH more painless, quick, and simple than you think it can.

We have reached the limits of where reason alone can take us. We don't need to rationalize and understand all the horrible things that happened to us, because - collectively - we have all come to understand that stuff already. It's NOT the 50's anymore, and we all basically understand - at the intellectual level - how the ways in which the world was cruel or unloving towards us hurt us and created patterns that we are still running from. An intellectual understanding of basic human psychology was essential in the evolution of our consciousness, but most of us have graduated to the next step now.

No amount of further understanding and analysis is going to help you truly release that reservoir of unresolved emotions. This is NOT an intellectual activity. Or... well... perhaps to be a little more fair and accurate, the intellectual part of this was just the beginning. It was the surface layer of healing meant to lead us towards a deeper journey. First, we needed to understand how disconnected to our emotions we were so that we could begin to move forward, but the next steps of this process must be done from within the heart. The pain exists in your heart, not your head, and we are going to need to shift our attention there. Learning how to speak the language of the heart so that we can release the pain of the past is what this shadow work journey is all about.

WHAT IS SHADOW WORK?

The first rule in any philosophical discussion is that we need to define our terms. Otherwise, how can we even know what we're talking about? So, let's make sure that we're all on the same page before we dive off into the deep end.

What is it that we mean when we say 'Shadow Work'?

Well, it is certainly an unclear term that is tossed around a lot and that has been interpreted in various ways, and - I suppose - there are actually various conceptions of what shadow work is and how to do it.

Shadow work was initially conceived of by Carl Jung (founder of modern Analytical Psychology) and it relates to his concept of the 'shadow' as being the unconscious aspects of the personality that the conscious ego no longer identifies itself with. Jung conceived of 'the shadow' as representing all the undesirable parts of ourselves that we had put away over the years and don't want to look at because they cause us emotional distress.

In Carl Jung's language then; shadow work is the process of reintegrating the undesirable shadow self back into the conscious ego self.

Now... I don't really like that definition for 2 main reasons.

Firstly, I feel like it's over-intellectualizing the fairly simple nature of the pain that we are trying to deal with at the core of shadow work. The phrase 'unconscious aspect of the personality' makes it seem like there is something that we need to consciously and intellectually rediscover about ourselves. It makes it sound as if there are logical answers that need to be found in order for us to be whole again, even though - as I have been trying to say - the real issue is just that we have blocked ourselves off from our emotions. The true problem is much simpler than this definition makes it seem.

It is true that there are unconscious elements of ourselves that need to be brought to light, but I find that this just confuses most people. It's much simpler to just talk about mastering our emotions. Both interpretations lead to the same place, but one makes sense to people immediately and the other makes the process seem more intellectual than it is. It's just over-complicated when it doesn't need to be.

Remember, Jung was operating during that time of our collective evolution where people needed to begin to understand the psyche at all. He had to approach things in a very academic way because people weren't ready to talk about their feelings so directly – as things in and of themselves. We have moved past that, though, and I find that this kind of definition is really dragging people backwards by now. The unconscious things that need to be revealed are simply our old patterns - the subconscious behaviors that we didn't used to notice. That's all. No further 'analysis' needs to happen. Only observation.

Secondly, I don't like the flowery and overly fancy language used because this simply pushes people further away from the truth. I think that overly-academic language is unhelpful for most people. To force people to overthink and over-intellectualize the process of reconnecting to our emotions is humorously ironic in my mind. It just pushes people to try even more to use their brains to solve this problem of the heart. It would be like me giving you a mathematical equation of how to cure anger. Even if the equation is correct, it's activating the wrong part of your brain for this kind of healing. The analytical side of you is not the part of you that's going to get you out of this emotional hole. It's only going to confuse you even more and prolong the true healing and release. It makes you think that you need to look right, even though the solution to your problem is only 2 steps to the left.

I especially hate the way the word 'ego' is thrown around by people who are starting to do this work, because no-one actually has any idea what they think they mean when they say that word. They've built up the 'ego' into this kind of boogie-man in their own heads. They believe that the 'ego' is some nasty part of themselves that itself is the villain of their story, which really just makes them believe that there are MORE undesirable parts of themselves that need to be put away. Our goal is to re-integrate all parts of ourselves, so when you tell yourself that your ego is an undesirable part of yourself, you're just causing more problems.

I just find that the overly-academic interpretation and approach is not helpful to people who are actually looking to do the healing. It's nice for a classroom discussion about why these methods work, but it is very distracting and confusing for those that are looking to learn how to heal right now.

I believe that what we are doing with shadow work is actually incredibly intuitive and very simple for absolutely anyone to understand when explained properly. In fact, I believe that what we are learning here is the most natural stuff in the world. I believe that these concepts will make immediate sense to a 7-year-old and can be expressed in language that a 7-year-old can grasp. You'll hopefully notice that this book is designed to be as easy to read as possible, because there is no-one who shouldn't be able to understand what we're talking about.

I wonder sometimes if I should really have a different term for my approach. I have wondered if perhaps my method of doing this inner healing varies enough from traditional Shadow Work methods that I should be using a term other than 'Shadow Work', but... in the meantime... I'm sticking with this term, and my interpretation of shadow work is as follows:

Shadow work is the process of learning how to observe, confront, heal, and release all of the uncomfortable emotions that we experience in any given moment - in a safe and healthy way - to allow us to finally release the unresolved emotions from the past that need to be released to keep us emotionally healthy and strong.

Or, to phrase it for the 7-year-old - Shadow work is about learning what to do with bad feelings when you have them so that they don't get stuck inside of you, and learning how to get rid of the bad feelings that were already stuck inside of you from the past. That's it!

We do this because as long as those feelings are stuck inside of us, we'll continue to be in pain and we'll continue to hurt ourselves and others. You can't run from something that's inside of you, so you have to face it and learn not to be afraid. There really is no reason to be afraid in the first place, anyway.

THE NATURE OF REPRESSED EMOTIONS

The human body has everything it needs to keep itself healthy, but we have forgotten how to tap into a lot of it.

Shadow work is the skill set of learning how to process and release the energies of fear, doubt, guilt, shame, anger, etc... that get built up inside of us. It is a method for resolving negative emotional frequencies so that they can be released and dissolved, instead of trapped and stored. It is the method of reconnecting to our truest selves by reintegrating the emotions that we have forgotten about through generations of repressing our human nature.

Just think of the uptight etiquette rules of high-class society where repressing our nature has essentially been the goal. Think of the tight, restricting clothing that women were forced to wear, the way men were taught to stuff down their emotions and the ways that we have all been repressing our base urges (like sexuality) in various periods and cultures of our collective societal developments. In an effort to appear to be civilized and to be more than base animals, we have shut down a lot of very essential aspects of our humanity, forgotten who we were and caused ourselves a lot of damage. If we simply connected to some of our more primal instincts, we would know how to release our negative energies immediately and instinctively and we would never need to do this thing that we now call 'shadow work'.

In the wild, after a gazelle escapes a predator, it will lie down and shake uncontrollably for a while. This is it's instinctive (and very effective) way of releasing the energy of fear that got built up inside of itself during the chase.[1]

The fear was helpful to the gazelle during the chase. It was evolutionarily beneficial. There was a literal physical danger and the fear provided endorphins and adrenaline to help the gazelle run faster, to escape this danger and survive.

Once it is out of danger, however, this fear energy no longer serves a purpose and needs to be released. Otherwise, the fear energy sticks around and starts to corrode the gazelle from the inside out. The gazelle will remain in constant fear to some extent from that moment on until this energy is released. It lives in a state of perpetual fear that there is always some predator chasing it. That fear will subside for brief periods and fly under the radar, but it's still there and the gazelle will get triggered into fear much more easily from that moment on.

Every moment of every day, the remnants of past trauma are trying to get released. The unresolved fear keeps trying to come up to get released for your own benefit, but it's still uncomfortable and you don't recognize that this is what's happening, so you stuff it back down. Your body will then use any event in your life that resonates with that

---

[1] There are healing modalities that try to mimic this, known as Trauma Releasing Exercises (or TRE).

unreleased emotion at all to try and remind you that the old pain is still there, waiting for you to deal with it.

And... THAT is what a trigger is!

A trigger is something that happens in your life that sparks an emotional frequency that resonates with stored emotions inside of you that never got released. Basically, the thing that triggers you in the present isn't your problem. The only real problem is that this trigger brought up an old emotion that you never dealt with, and your brain - not noticing this - attaches the old emotion to this new event and creates this self-perpetuating cycle where you keep bringing up old trauma just to stuff it back down.

To put that more simply, something that happens in your life brings up a small amount of anger in you. That small amount of anger activates the reservoir of trapped anger inside of you, making you get angrier than you needed to (I mean... you didn't need to get angry at all, but whatever). Your brain then thinks that this intense anger that you're feeling REALLY IS because of what happened to you right now (it doesn't recognize that it's just your past pain getting triggered), and so you never use this opportunity that your body just gave you. Your emotional body offered you a chance to heal by showing you your past pain but you turned your attention to the thing that triggered you instead. So, you stuffed the anger back down and piled this extra new problem on top of it. Your body gave you an opportunity to heal and you turned it down and turned it into just one more moment of unresolved emotional trauma that you'll need to deal with later.

Every moment of emotional distress that you experience presents you with that opportunity. Face it and heal, or stuff it down, run, and add an extra few liters of unresolved trauma to the reservoir of pain inside of yourself. You are always either moving up or down on this spiral staircase of emotional wellness.

What you don't realize then, is that a trigger is actually a GOOD THING! When you get triggered, it is because your emotional body is desperately trying to release this trauma energy from the past. This thing that's happening in your life right now creates a tiny instance of an emotion that is already trapped inside of you, and your emotional body is trying to connect you to that past pain because you still need to release it. It is trying to reconnect your pores to your sweat glands because this thing that is hurting you in the present moment is reminding your heart and your brain of the stuff that never had a chance to get released and expressed before.

There's past pain that exists inside of you, unresolved. That pain was created in a moment where you weren't safe to feel it, express it and release it... but now you ARE safe. You have been safe for a long time, but you never realized that, so you kept running from it. Your brain has constantly been under the impression that it is in danger, because your heart has been sending it these fear, doubt, guilt and shame signals ever since the initial trauma happened. Every time your heart had any opportunity to remind you of your past pain, it tried to - SO THAT YOU COULD HEAL, but you never recognized this, listened, or allowed the healing to take place.

Your heart is sending up this old pain to the brain, saying "hey... here's this pain you've been holding on to for 20 years, are you ready to feel it and deal with it?" and your brain says "no... I think I'm still in danger and I don't know how to safely feel those emotions, so cram it down... I'm not ready". The longer you've been stuffing this pain down, the more that you have stored up to clear so it just gets harder and harder with every passing year. I assure you though... it is NEVER too late!

Your emotional body has been trying to help you by connecting your surface level triggers to the buried pain inside of you, but you never learned how to make use of this evolutionarily crucial response to trauma that your brain has been trying to activate. Crying, for example, is a natural human response to trauma, but we have trained ourselves not to cry in a lot of cases. We have attempted to shut down our bodies' natural way of dealing with pain. So, the pain remains.

Unlike the gazelle, 'civilized' humans have forgotten how to naturally and safely release trauma energy. In fact, we didn't just forget! We actively programmed ourselves to shut that process down. We have over-intellectualized our own nature, and forgotten that we are - at our cores - emotional beings, and that our emotions need to be taken seriously and be dealt with appropriately and directly. The very nature of emotions is that THEY ARE NOT STRICTLY RATIONAL! So... what makes you think that a logical understanding of what caused your trauma in the first place is the ultimate solution to healing said trauma?

Yes... an understanding of this stuff is important to help get us to a certain point... but in order for true healing to take place, the process will need to be a little more holistic and intuitive.

Shadow work - then - is the process of learning what to do with negative emotions when they get triggered in us, so that we can use those moments to release the energy of a current and/or past trauma, to finally be free and clear of that energy.

Does that make sense?

Personally, I believe that this is a much more comprehensible and helpful explanation of what Shadow Work is than the academic Jungian understanding of the 'undesirable and repressed parts of our personality that need to be reintegrated'. Most people don't understand what that means (even if they think they do), but everyone can understand what 'stuffing down and not being in touch with your emotions' means.

WHAT IS THE GOAL OF SHADOW WORK?

The goal of shadow work is to rediscover the fullness of who we truly are. It is to release all of the fear-based programming that we have built up along the way to help us avoid feeling pain, so that we can start TRULY expressing ourselves again, and so that we can live in a more heart-centered fashion. What we don't realize along the way is that blocking ourselves off from pain necessarily forced us to block ourselves off from GOOD emotions also. You can't shut off the bad without also shutting off the good. We do shadow work to help us escape the low frequency of our unresolved pain and the cycles it created, and to open ourselves back up to the greatest emotions that this world has to offer and that our human bodies are capable of experiencing.

Ultimately, the goal of shadow work is 3 simple words... perhaps the most important words you will ever hear...

UNCONDITIONAL SELF LOVE!

That is what this journey is all about.

If you had nothing but those 3 words to guide you, you would be able to find your way.

In fact, it is those 3 words alone that started me on my path. Those 3 words were all I had to truly help me start navigating this path of inner healing.

The foundation of EVERYTHING that we are doing on this healing journey and everything we should be doing on this Earth MUST be unconditional self love. When you truly come to understand the depths and the intricacies of what those words really mean, they will lead you to a level of inner peace that most people in the western or modern world have never even stopped to consider or contemplate. To be living from true unconditional self love implies so much more than you are likely ready to understand.

There are a million ways in which we betray ourselves every day. You don't realize all the things you're doing every single day that cause you to be in more suffering and pain than you need to be. This includes all of the fear based emotional defense mechanisms that we have built up to protect ourselves from pain. You don't realize how often you are using them and how much pain and suffering they are causing in your life. You don't realize how you yourself are the main cause of most of your problems, and how your defense mechanisms are absolutely the cause of the vast majority of your suffering.

You yourself are perpetuating the cycles that keep you in pain... you just can't see it yet. You have not yet 'woken up' and raised your consciousness above those cycles enough to see them clearly.

Your life is completely in your own hands, and only by taking control of yourself in those ways can you start moving towards a better life for yourself, but most people spend their whole lifetimes playing the game the other way around.[2] They try to get their external lives in order so that they can feel good and safe first and then - if they are still not at peace - maybe they will look at their emotional wellbeing directly. Ie - you believe that when you have enough money in the bank, when you have the right home, the right relationship and the right car, THEN you will be able feel at peace, and only when you have all of those things but are still not happy will you bother to look inside and see what's wrong. You think that the reason you are suffering is external and you're trying to fix that first.

In fact, it is the complete opposite that is true. When you have learned how to master yourself and how to be happy in the moment regardless of what you may or may not have, THEN you will be in the best position to create the life that you want for yourself.

No amount of money can buy you inner peace, but inner peace can help lead you to make plenty of money - if that is still your goal once you have attained it - because people will pay to learn from you, or simply because you will have the strength of character, the determination, and the will power, etc... to turn whatever venture you strive to bring to life a success, and/or to pick yourself up time and time again after 'failures' until you eventually find what you are seeking.

Inner strength and mastery will always lead to outer success for those who seek it, but the opposite is hardly ever true. External success will NEVER lead you to inner peace, no matter how successful you become, but inner peace will always lead you to success. The best that external success can do is give you the time and sense of freedom to pursue inner healing more... but you didn't really need all that money to get started, you were just doing a better job of distracting yourself until you had all the things you thought you wanted and found that you

---

[2] It is only half true (at most) that your life is fully in your own hands. When we get to the higher levels of spiritual awareness there is a whole other discussion to be had about how you are not actually in control of your life at all, but... there are levels to our understanding and for now it's important that you start recognizing the ways that you ARE in control - or should be.

still weren't happy. You got to the end of the road on your left, only to finally realize that you should have gone right at the fork.

So, the overall goal is to achieve unconditional self love, where we are always acting in alignment with who we are, so that we can end this self-betrayal and inner conflict and start moving into a life that is founded on inner strength and self love, rather than fear, self-betrayal and cowardice of connecting to our emotions and expressing our true selves.

Unconditional self love will naturally lead us to learning unconditional love for others, because - as already mentioned - hurting someone else in fact hurts us at the emotional, spiritual and psychological levels. It is impossible for someone who truly loves themselves to be knowingly or intentionally cruel to another without also causing themselves pain. Therefore, to fully love oneself is also to fully love others unconditionally and to be kind and compassionate and understanding.

Yes... there are lines that need to be drawn and boundaries set up against behavior that doesn't serve us, but ultimately - for our own benefit - we must love others unconditionally. We must never betray ourselves in order to give unconditional love to another, but we must also never avoid giving unconditional love because doing so is a matter of self-betrayal. Unconditional self love requires unconditional love for others. It just requires that it's done in the right way (I'll discuss this more later in this book).

It is vitally important though to realize that the opposite is NOT true.

It is NOT the case that unconditional love for others naturally leads us to discover love for ourselves, and that is a cycle that many of us have been in for a long time. This is the reason that self love must be the foundation.

Many people suffer from being people-pleasers, or they keep slipping into savior syndrome or martyrdom, thinking that sacrificing their own well-being for the well-being of others is in fact the best and most moral thing to do. People try to cover up their own self-loathing by over-giving of themselves to others. Ultimately though, this just leads to them draining themselves and perpetuating negative, self-harming cycles that ultimately leave them empty and incapable of truly giving the best of themselves to anyone.

So, if your focus is on others first... you will ultimately find yourself drained and empty with nothing truly left to offer to others. While you are in this state, the love that you offer these people is not truly a solid unconditional love. It is faux-love. It is actually a cry for help from your inner self, desperately asking you to turn that love and energy that you are offering to the other person back onto yourself. Your subconscious is using this other person as a mirror, trying to get your attention onto your emotional wounds.

If unconditional love towards others is your golden rule, you will follow that rule until you kill yourself and no-one will really benefit in the long run. If you focus on self love though, once you are somewhat stable you will start focusing on how to love others unconditionally and in a healthy way because that is how you reach the next level of your own happiness and fulfillment. Then, everyone wins.

The logical outcome of unconditional self love is unconditional love for others because doing any less than that for others is just another way of betraying ourselves. Whereas the logical outcome of unconditional love for others - when unrestrained by unconditional self love - is self-destruction. So, we need to build everything on self love. For everyone's benefit, you MUST put yourself first!

WHAT IS SELF LOVE?

It's important to note that when we talk about 'self love' as being the ultimate foundation of everything we should do, we are referring to a deep level of self love that goes beyond the practical elements of our lives and our decisions. A lot of people think that self love ultimately leads to selfishness, but that's not at all true. It's really about us taking care of ourselves at the soul level so that we can be the best version of ourselves to give to the world. True self love will include the concept of being of service to others.

To try to put it as simply as possible, self love is about being in alignment with one's self. Self love is about eliminating the conflict that exists inside of us by making sure that all elements of our being are aimed in the same direction. There are various elements of your personality, but more importantly, various elements of your experience of reality, that are all trying to guide you in your life. When these elements are in alignment with each other, we can find inner peace and head in a solid direction with strength, force, and speed. When these elements are out of alignment, however, we spend every minute in inner conflict, trying to go in multiple opposing directions at once, which will only go to perpetuate negative cycles that will encourage that inner conflict to grow.

It turns out, we actually have 3 'brains'. Our heads, our hearts, and our guts. Each of these helps to produce a different element of our experience of reality - namely - our thoughts, our emotions, and our sensations.

[Ok... while the above statement is indeed true (scientists are aware that the heart and the gut operate with their own independent nervous systems and they are starting to recognize the '3 brains' and how they each play a role in our conscious experiences in subtle ways that we didn't realize before), I'm being slightly metaphorical here when I equate your 'heart brain' with your 'emotions' or your 'gut brain' with your physical sensations... So, don't worry so much about the minutiae of the biological details. The main point is that there are 3 overall elements to our experience of reality; our thoughts, our emotions, and our sensations. There is nothing that you can consciously experience that does not fall into one of those categories, and - for the sake of simplicity - from here on out, I will refer to these elements of your experience of reality as your heart (Cardiac Brain - emotions), your gut (Enteric Brain - sensations) and your actual brain (Cephalic Brain - your cognitive abilities and conscious thoughts).]

In order to achieve unconditional self love, we need to make sure that these 3 brains are all aimed in the same direction, but this is where things get tricky...

YOUR BRAIN IS AN ASSHOLE (AND A COWARD)

Our goal is to connect and align all 3 brains, but you've quite literally spent your entire life building up walls between them. We've already talked about this a little, but let's dive deeper into how we've built these walls in the first place.

When we first came into this world, we were nothing but light and love and joy and everything that is awesome in this world, but then we started experiencing trauma in our lives and this created pain at the emotional, spiritual, and sensational (physical sensations) level. This is when the brain clicked on and said, "WOAH!!! I am not enjoying this experience. I don't like this pain and I don't know what to do with it", and in that moment your brain did what it could to disconnect from the pain signals being sent to it from the heart and the gut.[3] It started

---

[3] Your initial traumas were NEVER rooted in your cognitive brain. It was never your intellect that was suffering. You were experiencing either emotional, spiritual or sensational pain. Never 'cognitive' pain. It was only as a result of this initial trauma that your brain formed the cognitive association between an event and some form of suffering that would be able to cause us cognitive pain later. Pain never begins there.

learning how to tune out from those signals and how to block them so that it didn't need to suffer in the moment.

This is the same way that pain-killers work, by the way. Instead of dealing with the source of the pain, they shut off the brain's pain receptors so that you don't feel it. The source of the pain is still there. Even the pain signals are still there. You have just turned off the part of you that understands how to feel it. You are disconnected enough from the source to not feel the pain coming from it and to not suffer because of it in a direct way. This is what your brain did with uncomfortable emotions and sensations. It learned how to shut off its pain receptors towards this kind of discomfort.

What happens, though, if you break your leg but you never do anything about it other than take pain killers? You'll completely destroy your leg by continuing to walk on it until it is completely useless and beyond repair, and that's what you've been doing with your emotional body. You haven't been healing your wounds. You've just been training yourself not to notice the pain, continuing to put stress and pressure onto an already injured part of yourself, making the problem worse day by day by ignoring a piece of you that needed healing.

So, your brain started creating the defense mechanisms that would slowly cause a complete divide between your conscious brain and your emotional body - in order to help you stay in control when you experienced emotional, spiritual, or physical distress and trauma.

Trauma didn't need to be anything extreme, by the way. Basically, anything that brought up frequencies of distress and fear in the moment counts as trauma. It could have been something as simple as telling one of your schoolyard friends that you liked a particular TV show and then having that friend tell you that they hate that show and that the show is stupid. Then, maybe, other kids started teasing you for it and it became a whole thing.

In that moment, your brain made an association. It recognized that when you opened up and expressed yourself honestly, sharing your passions and joys, that led to judgment, criticism and pain. Neurons fired down certain pathways simultaneously, creating a conscious and subconscious connection between the parts of the brain responsible for processing the various elements of the situation that just happened. In that moment, the parts of your brain responsible for self-expression were firing at the same time as the pathways for emotional distress, and so now your brain associates those two things as having a direct relationship, and since the emotion that you felt in that moment was strong, so is the association that your brain formed in that moment.

The brain's job is to then analyze the things that caused you pain in the past and calculate all the ways that they might happen again in the future. It can then help to determine a rational course of action that is most likely to help you avoid encountering the same scenario in the future. Its job is also to find ways of not feeling the pain when it comes to us so that we can survive our day to day lives in this 3D world and keep moving forward through the more practical aspects of our lives.

Hopefully, you can already see how this means that you are constantly acting from fear. Your brain has shut down its connection to the heart and the gut in order to avoid feeling the uncomfortable emotions and sensations that never got processed (it is afraid to allow those feelings through), and it is making all of its decisions based on the logic of "how to avoid potential future pain". Most major decisions that you have made have been founded on the reasoning of "I don't want to feel the emotional pain of the past ever again".

That is fear.

Your heart is always trying to push you in the direction of love, and your brain is - more or less - always pushing you in the direction of fear.

When we were in emotional or physical pain and we didn't know how to deal with it, we retreated to the cognitive parts of ourselves and tried to compartmentalize the various aspects of our experience. We created a divide inside of ourselves and a hierarchy where our heads needed to always be in control. God help us if we ever let our emotions show in public or were to truly be vulnerable with another human being. Our hearts and our guts couldn't handle that kind of true connection with another, because we had severed our connections inside of ourselves so much that our ability to process high intensity emotions - even the good ones - has been crippled.

With our heads in control and our conscious minds having completely forgotten what it actually once felt like to be in true alignment with oneself and living from the heart space, we continued to live these superficial versions of our own lives, until we completely lost track of the fullness of what being human is meant to feel like.

Fortunately, one by one... we all started experiencing this 'awakening' that - if you are reading these words right now - you are going through. The 'awakening' is a remembering of the fact that there is more to us than this cold, logical, intellectual, physical version of ourselves, and that the pleasures of the external world pale in comparison to the immense potential of inner joy that we can cultivate inside of ourselves.

Awakenings can be a lot of things, actually, but for now what we can agree on is that there are latent parts of yourself that are starting to come online again. That's why you're doing this work. You're slowly starting to remember, either at the conscious, subconscious, emotional or spiritual level that there used to be more to who you were or that there can be more to who you are, and you are looking to reconnect with all those lost parts of yourself.

In order to do that, like I said, we need to get our heads, our hearts, and our guts into alignment. If your heart is telling you to go one way and your brain wants you to go another, there is inner conflict and turmoil. This is - in my opinion - the actual root cause of anxiety, by the way. When our 3 brains are aimed in different directions, it creates a fairly literal storm within ourselves, the same way that a cold front and a warm front coming into contact with each other will cause intense weather shifts. The two cannot exist harmoniously in the same place and your body is trying to figure out what to do with these conflicting signals and energies, and that causes the looping thoughts and the turning feeling in the pit of our stomachs or hearts that we generally call anxiety.

When the 3 brains are out of alignment, the inner 'you' can't decide what to do. One part of you wants to go left, one part of you wants to go right, one part of you wants to just sit down and scream, and that inability to come to a conclusion - the torturous inner conflict between the battling parts of yourself - is what causes anxiety. When all of our brains are aimed in the same direction, however, anxiety disappears. I have seen this time and time again with my clients and in myself.

Here's the thing though...

Your brain is programmable. We spend every minute of every day training our brains. Every thought, every word, every action, everything that we see, hear, taste, etc... is shooting neurons down certain pathways in our brains and every time we shoot neurons down a certain pathway we help to pave that pathway, thereby training the brain to go down that same pathway again the next time. So, the things that you allow yourself to experience and to choose repeatedly start creating deeply entrenched pathways in your brain that slowly - and literally - program your personality and the way that you experience and process reality.[4]

Think of your brain like an open, fresh field of grass. If you walk through a field once, you'll barely leave a mark. But if you walk through it 10 times, 100 times, 10,000 times... eventually you start paving a clear pathway. Eventually, you'll pave a pathway so clear that you would

---

[4] This is why we need to be impeccable with our words and not speak judgment, slander, lies, etc... by the way. Because you are constantly paving pathways in your brain with every word you speak or think. See my other book '10 Mind Hacks for Quicker Emotional Healing' for more info on this. You can find that book on Amazon or some other online book retailers, or at http://benjysherercoaching.com/MHBook.

never even think to walk any other way through that field again. We will always naturally gravitate to the easiest path, in just the same way that water always flows to the lowest point. Without some reason not to, we will always choose the path of least resistance.

Eventually you will have completely forgotten that you were the one who paved that pathway in the first place, that the pathway could have been completely different, and that you can change and start building a new pathway any time you want to. You've become so accustomed to the old pathways that you're operating completely on auto-pilot, never bothering to realize or consider why you are walking that pathway to begin with.

Now that you're starting to wake up and recognize the self-harming nature of your old pathways, you finally have a high enough state of consciousness - and the proper motivation - to start taking control of your subconscious cycles and to start paving new pathways.

But... paving a new pathway can't happen in an instant. You had to walk down that old path 10,000 times to pave it. Now it's going to take 10,000 times to pave the new one, while you fight the urge to keep walking down the old, easier, pre-paved pathway. So, please recognize that this is all a process. Don't expect one giant switch to flip over at any one instance and have all your problems slip away. Just realize that at any given moment you can choose to start walking a different path. Every time you go for a walk (metaphorically), you will need to choose to put in the extra effort to start paving that new pathway, and every time you DO choose that, you pave the new pathway a little more and you let the old one grow over a little bit.

When you make the grand decision to change, sometimes you'll remember to walk the new path and sometimes you'll walk the old one because you're still getting used to the new way and/or because you slipped back into auto-pilot mode for a moment. There will be some back and forth while you start making this transition and that's fully ok. If you give yourself crap for not being perfect with your new habits immediately, you will just create a shame cycle that will keep you in your old pathways even longer.[5]

---

[5] Once again, you can find more info on this in my other book '*10 Mind Hacks for Quicker Emotional Healing*'. You can read more about this shame cycle and how to avoid it in the chapter titled "Give Your Brain a Cookie". More info at http://BenjyShererCoaching.com/MHBook.

POWER OF THE HEART

So, our brains are being programmed every minute of every day, every single time we shoot neurons down a given pathway.

Our hearts, on the other hand... CANNOT be programmed! The heart knows what it knows and wants what it wants and that's all there is to it. You can't force the heart to love someone or something it doesn't love and you can't force it to stop loving something that it already loves (trust me... I've tried). The heart is much more connected to external frequencies and is far more intuitive than you realize. It knows things that can't be expressed to the brain. It doesn't operate with the same kind of programmable neural connections that the brain does, so it cannot be trained in the same way.

So, we have spent our lifetimes programming our cephalic brains (head brains) to stay in control in ways that are in complete misalignment with the part of ourselves that CANNOT be programmed (your emotions - heart brain). That means that your heart has been spending your lifetime desperately trying to make you go right, and you have spent your lifetime programming your brain to go left. Your heart kept yelling and yelling "RIGHT!!!!" because your heart can NEVER be at peace unless you move in that direction, and your brain... too afraid to face the emotional pain that's blocking the path on your right... kept ignoring that and saying "left".

So, you went left. Over and over and over. You ignored the part of you saying "right" for so long that you completely forgot how to hear it and what its voice actually sounds like; because this is a voice that you need to PRACTICE hearing. Your heart speaks a different language than your brain and if you don't keep practicing that language of emotion you forget how to speak it.

Your emotional brain has been locked away for a long time, yelling at someone who isn't listening and who doesn't even speak its language anymore. An 'awakening' is about that voice getting louder and louder, and you not being able to ignore it anymore - even though you currently don't really know how to listen to it or understand it. Right now, it's just this frustrating background noise behind everything you do. It's an underlying uncomfortable feeling that follows you everywhere you go because you know that something isn't quite right with the way that you are living your life. It's like having a stranger follow you around yelling at you in Chinese all day long.

As you train yourself to listen to it, trust it, and follow it, though... everything else will become clear, and that 'background noise' that's driving you insane right now turns into beautiful heavenly music guiding you on every step of your life and journey. Slowly, you start to understand what that Chinese person is saying, and it opens you back up to a larger version of who you once were. You used to speak Chinese... you just forgot.

Now, if we want to get these 3 brains into alignment, we are going to have to realize that since we cannot program our hearts, we are going to need to program our brains instead, to be in alignment with what the heart wants. Our hearts NEED to go right, but our brains can be trained to go in any direction. So, the only way to make sure that both are always moving in the same direction is to program our brains to follow our hearts (rather than silencing our hearts in order to follow our brains, which is what we have been doing so far).

And that, my friends, is the simple truth in all of this.

Our hearts are the core of who we are and our hearts need to be leading the way. If they are not given the reigns to lead, then we will necessarily be in conflict within ourselves and that's all there is to it. In order to achieve self love, the heart is going to need to be in control. This means that we desperately need to learn how to speak the language of the heart again. This is why shadow work is not an intellectual activity - because the whole point is that we are trying to reactivate the part of ourselves that doesn't speak the same language as the intellect. Your brain is speaking to you in English, your heart is yelling at you in Chinese. You won't be able to help the Chinese man until you learn to speak his language. I.e. you can't solve a problem of the heart by speaking the language of the head. You can't heal your emotional wounds with logic.

It's time for your brain to retire. It can go play shuffleboard and bingo on the beach in Florida. The next stage of our evolution, our self-actualization and of our consciousness can only be achieved through the heart and we need to learn how to speak the unconscious language of emotions in order to get there.

GETTING BACK
TO THE HEART

So, what is it going to take for us to reconnect with our hearts and reprogram our brains to surrender to the path that the heart wants to take?

Basically, it's going to be a process of learning how to confront uncomfortable emotions. Step by step and in a safe manner, of course. Overall, it is going to be a process of confronting and eliminating fear. Now that we are no longer in the danger that we were in when the initial traumas created those fear based pathways in our brains, we are going to need to learn and to realize that we are safe to finally feel all of that unpleasant stuff that wants to run through us.

The problem is that there is a lifetime's worth of pain that is currently trying to work its way through a heart that has been ignored and stuffed away for who knows how long. Your heart is (metaphorically) a muscle that needs to be exercised. You need to practice listening to it and connecting with it in order to train it to be able to handle heavier and heavier emotions. This is what it means to be emotionally healthy and strong. To be able to experience intense

Lotions and maintain self awareness during times of emotional distress (or intense emotional pleasure, for that matter). To be able to feel the most intense emotions possible without losing ourselves in those moments and doing something that will cause more problems.

In order to do that, we will need to clear away all of the unresolved emotions that are stuck inside of us (because those are the things that get triggered that push us to react poorly and enter these negative, self-harming cycles), but we can't just start diving into the worst things that happened to you right away. You're not ready for that big stuff! Your heart isn't strong enough yet!

The core wounds that first happened to you that set all of this stuff in motion in the first place are like the 200-pound weights of emotional distress inside of you. Plus, those heaviest weights are currently buried under a lifetime's worth of other weights, and right now... you're not even strong enough to lift 5 pounds because no-one has ever shown you how to do so properly. You've never learned how to confront the little triggers that come up and how to deal with your small uncomfortable emotions in a healthy way, so what makes you think that you're prepared to dive into all of your worst childhood trauma and release your pain that way?

It's just not going to happen.

It would be like walking into a gym and saying to the physical trainer, "Hey... I'd like to lift 500 pounds today. I don't want to work out or train for years, I'd like you to just show me how to lift 500 pounds right now, and once I do that, I'll never have to come back into the gym again."

There are so many reasons why things just don't work that way.

But that's actually the good news! The healing journey is not about 'chasing down traumas' or 'seeking out your demons'. You don't need to go actively searching for this stuff. You don't need to trace it to its source and analyze it. You don't need to piece it all together or understand it.

You don't need to focus on the negative at all, actually. You don't need to push yourself to lift any more than you are ready to at any time.

Instead, your goal is simply to learn how to feel as good as possible as often as possible and to learn how to confront the uncomfortable emotions that are constantly coming up inside of you, naturally. By starting with the small ones, you will build the shadow work muscle and slowly start undoing the layers of fear-based programming. You will get stronger and stronger at handling anything uncomfortable that comes your way. You will learn to surrender, to release and to allow uncomfortable emotions to flow through you because you will no longer be afraid to feel them. You will finally release your resistance to all the things that need to express themselves.

Think of it like this; your heart has constantly been sending these emotional pain signals up to your brain. Since you didn't know how to deal with them and didn't want to feel them, your brain initiated its natural 'pain killer' response. It tensed up and shut down all the pathways between your head and your heart and that's how it avoided pain. Now, all you need to do is relax and open up those pathways again with the knowledge that you're not in danger anymore and that these outdated pain signals that need to be processed can't actually hurt you.

To put it another way, it's as if - at every moment of emotional distress that you ever experienced - you produced a single liter of 'trauma energy' inside of you, and every liter of trauma energy inside of you needs to be released (sort of like 'calories in and calories out' for a diet) by getting experienced and processed through your conscious experiencing of it. Every bit of trauma energy that has ever been created needs to be released, and the way to release it is to allow yourself to feel it. Once you allow this unpleasant emotion to fully run through you it will disappear, but you are going to need to open up and let this happen.

It will be uncomfortable at times, but it will also be awesome. When you let go of fear, all that's left is ease, bliss, love, and joy. Confronting your demons can be painful... but it can't actually hurt you, and that's

53

the real secret. When you truly realize that, the whole notion of 'suffering' changes.

The emotions that you've been running from your whole life can't actually hurt you! They absolutely do not have the capacity to. They are intangible. They have no form. They have no real way of persuading you into anything. They have absolutely no impact on the real world except the power that you give them by resisting them. In fact, the only things that can hurt you are the actions that you keep taking to help you avoid feeling the emotions that are trying to run through you. The emotions themselves (though 'painful' at times) cannot actually harm you in any way. Fully allowing yourself to feel them can't cause you any harm. Running from them, on the other hand, does cause you harm. Every time.

This is one of the reasons we call it 'shadow work', because it's literally like trying to run away from your own shadow. Futile, frustrating, and painful.

Your shadow is attached to you. You literally can't run away from it. It defies logic to try to do so, and it would be a completely futile endeavor. You will never escape it because it only exists as a function of your relationship with light. You will always have a shadow so long as you are standing in the light. So, if you spend your life afraid of your shadow, you will always be in peril and life will be torturous, with never a moment's rest from that predator.

If, on the other hand, you were ever to just stop running from your shadow and actually stop and look at it for a moment, you'd realize that it never had any capacity to hurt you. There was never anything to be afraid of and run from at all. Your shadow was never a threat, but your fear of it led to ongoing suffering that you couldn't escape from. ONLY your fear was causing you pain, and only when you stop running can you finally be at peace, but so far, you've never allowed yourself to stop and see that because you've convinced yourself that your shadow wants to kill you.

So, your shadow is every uncomfortable thought, feeling, belief, or memory that you were never willing to stop and sit with in the past. All the pain that you told your emotional self to hold onto because you weren't ready to deal with it. Your brain still thinks that you're in danger and so it doesn't want you to look at these things - lest you let your guard down for a moment and the imaginary predator pounces - but we are going to need to let our guards down so that we can finally heal. We are going to need to convince our brains that we are safe, so that we can finally stop resisting the signals being sent to us from our hearts.

The more that you let go and surrender to this process without fear and with a firm understanding of why this is just how the healing process goes, the more painless it becomes. Remember, the emotions can't hurt you, only your fear and resistance to them cause you actual pain and harm, and in order to finally heal and live your best life, all that you need to do is let the unresolved emotions finally move through you. You have been resisting the very thing that could make your life better, and only by resisting it have you been in pain.

Do you see what I mean about the deep layers of self-betrayal you've been under?

The 8 Steps

Now that we know what shadow work is, why we do it, and some of the intricacies and common misconceptions and mistakes around it, the obvious question presents itself...

"Ok... so... how do we go about accomplishing this already? How do we actually shift out of our heads and into our hearts? How do we eliminate fear and learn to live freely, truly, and authentically as ourselves?"

Well, I have good news and bad news for you. Let's start with the good news!

The good news is that I am going to tell you exactly how to do it. In just a moment, I'm going to run you through the full 8 step process that I use with all my clients to get them through this transformational period in their lives and into their new selves, with newfound strength, confidence and vigor for life, in record timing. How we completely shift them from that negative spiral and onto a positive spiral, free of fear, as quickly and painlessly as possible. You will - hopefully - understand how when we put these 8 steps together, properly and truly mastered, there is nothing left to fear anymore. You will get the best and most detailed overview that I can manage in a book like this, to show you the path that needs to be followed and I will do my best to hold nothing back and to give you as much guidance as possible.

The bad news is that this book alone cannot truly get you to the finish line... for a lot of reasons.

Firstly, and most importantly, just as I've been saying that the problem is not intellectual but rather emotional, so is the process of doing this healing not intellectual but emotional and practical. By reading this book you will have a phenomenal foundation of information and an excellent intellectual understanding of what you need to do and why... but that alone cannot give you all the results... because you need to actually PRACTICE this stuff, train with it and build these muscles directly and consciously to experience the kinds of shifts you are hoping to experience through shadow work.

You can read all the books about swimming that you like and gain a phenomenal understanding of the strokes and the muscles involved and all the mechanics of what it takes to swim, but until you get in the water you are never going to truly learn what it feels like to be in there and you will never be able to start training the muscles and developing the muscle memories that need to be established so that your body can get into a groove and accomplish what you intellectually know that it can.

If you want to be a MASTER swimmer, then you are going to need to train at it for who knows how long.

Now, an intellectual understanding of this stuff is in fact where we need to start. We can't truly just start working from the heart when we have spent our lives so far living entirely from the head. If we can't make ourselves intellectually aware of WHY and HOW we want to learn to work from the heart and what that means, then we won't even be aware of what we need to do and we won't be able to start. Our journey starts in the head, but the goal is to get into the heart.

Level 1 is about intellectually comprehending the unconscious and harmful cycles we've been in this whole time... but then, for level 2, we are going to need to move past the intellect and connect to the very part of ourselves that defies it. When we learn to tune back into the heart, we will then start to understand more about ourselves intellectually as well, but we are going to need to feel it before we can understand it. I.e., there are certain misconceptions you'll have about swimming if you only learn from a book that you'll only be able to fix once you get a real trainer and get into the water (there are certain things that must be felt and experienced in order to be learned).

Secondly, I am about to provide you with the best outline possible for a solid framework that you are going to need to follow to heal... but this is just the framework. I certainly don't have the space in a book like this to go into all the deep ins and outs; every exercise, method, and tactic we use in order to accomplish this or all the deep wisdom behind all of those things.

To the truly astute among you, this book has already given you more than everything you need to know to accomplish all of this on your own. In fact... as I already mentioned, when I started my true healing and ascension journey I had nothing but 3 words to guide me that I have already given you - Unconditional Self Love. These are the words that led me in my direction and taught me everything I needed to know. Through a true and deep understanding and embodying of this concept of unconditional self love, all other healing can be accomplished. So, I've already given you way more than everything you need.

Most of you didn't spend your lives searching for these answers and training your philosophical minds to search through this maze of your inner selves the way I did, though... and that's why I'm here to share this wisdom with you.

To be honest, even to those 1 in a million amongst you who could find your way through this maze alone, I can say this... You have no idea what I would have given to have someone who could have shown me the way as I am trying to do for all of you. The absolute hardest part of this journey is figuring out how to actually do the healing. With the right road map and the right support and guidance, this journey can be so much simpler and make so much sense. Even if you are destined to lead, that doesn't mean that you have to get there all on your own. Take the hand that is being offered to you when you have the chance. I truly wish I had someone who could have explained to me what I am going to explain to all of you.

The whole reason people like me need to find the path of this journey on our own is so that we can show it to others. Most of you don't need to go through the same trial and error that I did, because you have in fact found me, and because - more and more every day - more lightworkers are emerging to guide others with the distinct divine blueprint that they carry, in order to help the rest of the world through the same awakenings and healings we had to carve our own ways through. You don't need to invent the wheel, because someone else already did.

Each one of us carries a certain blueprint - the imprint of our souls translated into the physical world - that we came to share. This *Feelings First Shadow Work* approach is part of my blueprint. I recognize that now. I recognize how this wisdom has always been inside of me. It's just who I am. It's easy for me to see now how my whole life relates to this wisdom and the opportunity to share it. My entire personality was just hovering around this knowledge, a constant reflection of that seed of wisdom that was waiting to sprout out of me.

The challenge, for all of us, is to work on ourselves enough to expose - from underneath all the human, 3D, programmed nonsense - that divine blueprint. You don't need to become anything or 'learn' anything really... you simply need to expose that core of who you are by eliminating all of the fear-based programming on top of it. Most people are so busy playing the Earth game though, that they don't dive into the emotional and spiritual work necessary to reveal that truest sides of themselves, and never experience true self-expression, fulfillment, or inner peace. You, on the other hand, are on the inner journey to getting there! Good for you! If you stick with me, I'll show you exactly how to uncover that core nugget of yourself and bring your divine blueprint to the world.

The blueprint that I have to share will help many, and other lightworkers have other blueprints that will help others.[6] There is not 'One Way' through this healing. There are many. And different teachings resonate with different people, and that's not only fine... it's beautiful. We all came from different places to end up at the same destination. That's awesome.

If you are here reading these words and appreciate all I have been sharing with you so far, I would like to pause and thank you from the bottom of my heart. To know that my words have an impact... to know that my divine blueprint and the wisdom I carry inside of me is what will help you move forward into the next stage of your life - even if in just a small way - is truly beautiful. It means that I am truly living and fulfilling my life's purpose, and that is a magical feeling. Also, if you are

---

[6] People sometimes misunderstand or over-estimate this term 'lightworker'. Some people definitely see it as a spiritual thing, denoting something about the path that their soul took to get this Earth lifetime. Some people see it as meaning that they - in the higher dimensions - actively volunteered to come to Earth at this time to help with the collective awakening that is happening right now. To be honest... I believe that. I believe that we are going through a very important shift in consciousness right now and that I volunteered to be here to help. I know people who actually remember being on the other side, before birth. But... to put it as simply as possible and to remove any spiritual connotation, a 'lightworker' is merely a person who feels a particular urge and calling to be of service to humanity and to help us evolve and grow in the direction of love and unity. Simple as that. Anyone who feels as if their duty in this life is to help us come together and who takes steps to fulfilling that duty is a lightworker. I am a lightworker. The title doesn't matter at all, but it helps people understand their personalities a bit and that can be very helpful as you struggle to figure out your identity in this life, and especially while you go through the beginnings of your awakening.

still here resonating with these words, then I can more or less guarantee that MY methods will work for you. You wouldn't have made it this far otherwise and if you commit to healing with me, I can get you to the other side faster than anyone else, because NO-ONE else teaches MY divine blueprint.

Like I said, though... I can give you only the framework and foundation here, and a head start. If you want to truly get through this journey, you will need to commit to putting in the work. I can help you get there in record timing and with as little pain as possible, but this book is just a start.

If you would like me to take you by the hand through this journey and lead you step by step through every exercise and explanation that you will need, then you can check out my 8 week course which follows the exact blueprint that I am going to lay for you here. We leave no stone unturned and we make sure that by the end of 8 weeks you have seen a massive transformation and are no longer reliant on me or anyone else to continue your healing and to step into the best version of yourself. If you are committed to unleashing the true and full version of yourself as quickly and painlessly as possible, that course is how we will do it.

You can find more info about the course at

http://BenjyShererCoaching.com/ffcourse.

The course used to be called *From Awakening to Ascended*, but after publishing this book it will probably just be *Feelings First Shadow Work - 8 Weeks to Emotional Mastery*. I cannot recommend this course enough. The transformations I have seen have been nothing short of miraculous. I'll tell you a bit more about that later on.

With no further ado... let's jump into the 8 steps to Self Love and Shadow Work.

STAGE 1 - THE HEALING

Step 1 - Foundation and Stability

Knowing that Unconditional Self Love is the ultimate goal (inner alignment between our 3 brains towards full self-expression and realization) and that shadow work is the method through which we accomplish this (the methods of how to confront, observe, and heal the uncomfortable emotions that arise in us at any given moment), we have the path laid out for us. We understand that it is into our fears that we need to journey, but... before we do that, we need to take a minute and stabilize ourselves.

We have to prepare for the journey. We need to prepare ourselves emotionally and make sure we are starting off on the right footing, and we also need to prepare ourselves intellectually to understand our relationship with our emotions, so that we can start to recognize our patterns, notice them, and face them more productively.

So, the first thing that we need to do as we begin this journey is to make sure that you are strong enough to do it. We need to know that you are not going to get lost in the darkness as you start wandering through the shadows.

We don't want to push you into the deep end of shark infested waters before we've even taught you how to swim!

It may sound simple and obvious, but trust me... it's not. It's simple and obvious to you right now because we're talking about it and because I started off by pointing this out, but I'd put money on it that you would have skipped this step doing it on your own... and that you HAVE been skipping this step over and over and over as you've tried to confront your problems so far. Most likely, this book is not your first investigation into inner healing, but also - most likely - you have never taken the time to develop or even understand what a solid emotional foundation is.

Be honest... if I hadn't started by saying 'the first step is to build a foundation', is that really what your answer would have been if I asked you, 'where do we start'?

So far, you've been acting from the brain and from fear. We all have been. It's our natural response to millennia's worth of passed down trauma and to the trauma that we ourselves experienced in our lives. That cognitive part of you is the part of you that's anxious to just dive into your wounds and to try and heal everything right away. It wants you to take action immediately! Just get it done! It knows what it wants to do and it just tries to dive right on in and force the outcome that it wants into reality. It's the "Go! Go! Go! DO! DO! DO!" part of you.

That's the intellectual and fear based part of you trying to solve the internal problems in the same way it has always been trained to solve external problems. With more action! With more rationality! With more hustle and grind!

So, how many times have you tried 'taking action' against your emotional issues versus how many times have you put serious effort into just developing good emotional habits first? We all want the solution to an anxiety attack in the moment but don't really put in the effort to change our lifestyles to help us avoid and prevent those anxiety attacks in the first place. We're entirely reactionary and never preventative when it comes to our emotions, until our lives crumble and/or we have an awakening. We tend to only respond to pain that we are having, rarely working on strengthening ourselves against pain in general to avoid suffering altogether.

If you don't prepare for this journey emotionally and intellectually, and stabilize yourself before you start, then you end up just diving into all of your past traumas, head first, with no idea of what to do with them even if you caught them and not yet strong enough emotionally to do it, even if you did know. Then you spend your day-to-day life in the emotional pain from which you're trying to escape in the first place and you're spending your off time focusing on all your pain from the past. You end up just bouncing back and forth between your daily emotional distress and your unresolved emotional distress and everything just seems awful.

No-where along the way have you actually stopped to develop any tools and techniques to help you cope with the emotions that are going to come up during this healing (remember, you will need to feel it to heal it). You've just developed an intellectual habit and routine of focusing on past pain to go along with the main dish of the emotional distress that you are already feeling every day. It's only going to make you feel worse, leave you more depressed and make you incredibly discouraged about this whole 'emotional healing' idea altogether.

So, our first step is to build this solid emotional foundation and make sure you're on a strong footing and going in the right direction.

1A - Understanding Emotional Cycles

Firstly, you need to understand a little bit more about your emotions. There are subconscious cycles that have been happening your whole life that have been perpetuating the programming that you developed as a trauma response and you need to come to understand this a little so that you can start noticing and observing these cycles when they start happening. Simply by observing a thought pattern, you interrupt it and provide the opportunity to consciously reverse it or - at least - to acknowledge it. This is the first step towards true change... observation.

Gaining this awareness and higher perspective on our previously unconscious cycles is, at its most basic, what 'raising your consciousness' means. Bringing to your conscious attention things that used to go unnoticed. What this 'awakening' is about is raising your consciousness above your emotions. Being able to - as often as possible - maintain awareness of your emotions and an understanding of your relationship with them, so that we can stop being triggered by them, so that we can master them, and so that we can unite more of the faculties and abilities we carry inside of us in order to experience more. To do more. To be more.

By raising our consciousness above our emotions and above the subconscious cycles that have been looping and perpetuating our own self-harming beliefs and behavior, we can finally take control of them and experience true change.

There is a subconscious cycle that has been happening your whole life between your head, your heart, and your gut (thoughts, emotions, and sensations), and this subconscious cycle has been controlling every decision you've ever made. You thought that you were making decisions based on logic and good reason, but you were actually being guided by the patterns happening beneath the surface of how these three parts of your reality were interacting - you just didn't recognize this because of all the work you had done building up walls inside of yourself.

Each of your 3 brains is playing an active role in creating the whole of your reality, and they are in constant communication with each other, sending signals and information back and forth. Initially, these signals were being sent freely in all directions, from all 3 brains in a glorious equilibrium, but over our lifetimes we have trained ourselves and programmed ourselves to speak, act and think in certain ways that have created a very particular flow - and a lack of flow - in various directions.

We learned to prioritize the cognitive brain and to push aside our emotions, our sensations and our instincts so often that this has become our base programming and we never noticed it. We think that 'the way we are' is just the way we are. We think that fear is innately programmed and that anxiety is our natural state that needs to be overcome in some drastic ways. We think that humans are naturally prone to evil and greed, etc... We think these things, but we don't realize that this is simply the programming that we have allowed to be installed into ourselves over generations because we never knew any better and hadn't yet raised our consciousness high enough to see and recognize these self-harming patterns.

We were unconscious to these behaviors. We were 'asleep'. We were passively letting our brains be programmed into negativity, instead of actively taking control and actively programing them for healing, growth, evolution and love. We didn't realize that we could take control of the subconscious programming of our brains, and so we let the world program us instead.

So, over our lifetimes we trained ourselves to consciously act only from our cognitive functions first and to block off the flow of information between our heads and our hearts. Of course, this was an illusion. We deceived ourselves into thinking that we were 'just acting logically' when really, we were actually acting in ways that helped us avoid feeling our unresolved emotions, which means that those unresolved emotions have in fact been in control of our lives. The more that you subconsciously tried to avoid your emotions, the more that it means that all of your decisions were actually a product of the emotions you were trying to avoid. All day long, your heart was trying to get your attention, and you kept looking the other way. Your unwillingness to look at your emotions was the ultimate decision making factor.

The heart would send signals to the brain about the emotional distress that we were in at any given moment and we've spent the majority of our lives training our brain to deal with emotional distress by shutting down access to the heart, and searching for the external thing that is causing this emotional reaction. The brain knows that its job is to find and solve an external problem that is causing your emotional distress whenever you feel any, and so it shuts down the connection to the heart in order to maintain the focus and energy to do that job. It stores away the emotional trauma in that moment and puts its focus onto the outside world to try to solve the trigger.

In moments of true and legitimate trauma, this was the right move. It was true that - in that moment - allowing yourself to process those emotions would have put you in more danger and not allowed you to tackle the real 3D problem, but this is for moments of legitimate trauma only, not your day-to-day life and frustration. This is only a proper response when you are actually in danger. Now, you're not in danger, but you've programmed this into your brain as your go-to response for emotional distress. Whenever something is bothering you emotionally, your brain believes that you are in danger and so it stuffs away the emotional pain to the best of its abilities and searches for the external problem and tries to solve that.

That is 'Protocol Alpha for Dealing with Emotional Distress' in your brain's current operating manual: Any time I sense emotional distress, I will shut down my emotional sensors, search for an external problem, and attempt to solve it. I will not turn my emotions back on until I am out of danger!

Aaaaand... Here's the REAL secret!

What do you think your brain does when it receives the signals of emotional distress and doesn't immediately find a problem in the outside world to attach that emotional distress to?

IT MAKES ONE UP!

Your brain desperately needs to stay in control of this situation because it knows that in the past - when it didn't - it led to more pain and struggle. Your brain is a coward who is absolutely desperate to avoid any pain, and so... when it doesn't find an immediate problem to solve (in hopes that solving a problem will solve your emotional distress) it imagines a problem so that it can perform its function. Otherwise, it feels helpless and powerless and it freaks out. If there is no 'problem', then it is forced to feel the emotions that it's trying to avoid. So, it chooses something in the external world that it can work on so that it can believe that it's performing its function of keeping you safe (not realizing that it's actually making the emotional problem worse by forcing you to see external problems where there aren't any).

Your brain's training says to solve an external problem in any moment of emotional distress, and it will insist on doing this even if it can't find a real problem to work on. Think of all the times you've randomly felt anxiety, anger, or sadness and spent time trying to figure out where it's coming from. You were trying to find a reason for your distress, even though there was no external reason to begin with. You wanted a logical explanation of why you were feeling emotional distress because finding an explanation (you thought) would allow you to take action to solve the emotional problem.

You were determined to find an external cause for your suffering, because the idea that "it just is" leaves you with no potential course of action and that's very uncomfortable when you don't understand what's happening. Your brain wants to look outside of you for problems, because external problems mean that there are external solutions. This is how your brain has learned to deal with your pain.

Now, in moments when you're not truly in danger but your past pain is getting triggered by something happening in your life right now, your heart is sending your brain messages of "I'm here now! It's safe! Please deal with these old distress signals I'm sending you! You promised me that you'd look at these things when you were safe!"

Every time your brain receives those messages it goes, "OKAY! Emotional distress! I know what to do with emotional distress! Let's crack into action and look for the problem outside of ourselves to fix!". The brain snaps into its programmed protocol and gets moving while the heart face-palms itself and shakes its head because you just went in the wrong direction.

So, the brain searches for a problem outside of itself and finds one even though none truly exist, and then it drives itself crazy trying to find a rational and logical solution to a problem that can't be rationalized or logically worked out, because we can't control everything in our lives in that way and because the problem was imaginary in the first place.

Even if we do manage to solve the imaginary problem that we just created in our heads, it won't help... because that wasn't the real problem! This is why external success will never lead to inner peace. Lack of external success was never the real problem. This was never why you lacked inner peace to begin with. The real problem was just the trapped, unresolved emotions inside of you that never got released and that are trying to get your attention right now. The real problem was your fear of allowing yourself to feel and process the emotional distress signals that your heart was sending up to your brain. Nothing else. So, no action other than learning to listen to our hearts can actually solve this problem. Anything else is just a distraction.

Then, the gut comes into the equation as you start experiencing physical distress in relation to this emotional trigger (and 'energetic' distress - like anxiety).[7] Due to our heads and hearts trying to push us in opposite directions and due to the overexertion of our conscious minds trying to solve a false problem, we experience all sorts of physical or other 'sensory' discomfort. Tense muscles, high blood pressure,

[7] The reason I refer to anxiety as 'energetic' discomfort is to help express that what I mean by 'sensory' is not necessarily physical. Yes... you can sometimes point to that turning feeling in the pit of your stomach that you call anxiety, but that turning feeling is not something that's physically happening that can be seen - for example - on an MRI or X-ray. It's important to note that 'sensation' doesn't only mean strictly 'physical'; that you can 'feel' things that aren't actually physically observable or measurable.

tightness in the chest, stomach acid, fatigue, insomnia, anxiety, panic attacks, ticks and twitches, etc... These are all sorts of unpleasant sensory experiences and physical reactions that we have as a result of this inner turmoil and self betrayal. This is how the gut is related to the heart and the brain, it translates our cognitive and emotional states into sensory experience.

These unpleasant sensory experiences that we have as a result of unpleasant emotions create more fearful thoughts (because we become worried about the sensory discomfort and are trying to avoid and ignore it), and then those fearful thoughts cause more uncomfortable emotions, which cause more uncomfortable sensations, and more uncomfortable thoughts... and around and around and around we go.

Thoughts > Emotions > Sensations > Thoughts > Emotions > Sensations.

That, in short, is the primary subconscious cycle that we need to be able to truly understand and start to notice. Those 3 elements of our experience of reality have been triggering each other non-stop, but we never noticed this and so we never learned to take control of it and reverse the flow from a negative spiral, into a positive one. The more that we can train ourselves to notice when this cycle is at play inside of us, the more quickly that we can interrupt this cycle and start to replace it with positive programming.

This cycle has been happening automatically and on auto-pilot, reinforcing negative pathways and harmful habits and beliefs, but we can take control of this cycle and start actively programming our brains for positivity and growth. We can learn how to take advantage of the ways that our brains naturally program themselves and start using these mechanisms to hack our brains for our benefit. We can start learning tricks to push our conscious or subconscious minds to perform certain actions or form certain connections. (Thus, the title of my other book, *10 Mind Hacks for Quicker Emotional Healing*).

By learning about how these subconscious cycles work, we bring our passive unconscious programming to our conscious mind's attention, thereby interrupting the old thought patterns so that we can replace them with new positive programming that will help us heal and improve our lives. We will begin to turn every moment of emotional distress into a moment of raising our conscious awareness and of healing unresolved wounds. Every trigger becomes an opportunity to heal! They are no longer anything to fear and run from.

Once you have learned to notice and interrupt those patterns, your mind becomes more awake and ready to heal. You are raising your consciousness high enough above your internal cycles to begin to see them clearly and to start bringing the unconscious behaviors to the surface so that you can finally escape them. You are escaping the fear of confronting the uncomfortable emotions that are constantly arising in you because you understand the illusion of them, their inability to hurt you, the way they act as clues to your inner growth and the self-harm involved in succumbing to their illusions and stuffing them away.

1B - Emotional Boot Camp

While we prepare our minds and wrap our heads around this concept of subconscious cycles, we must also prepare our hearts for this journey. We need to make sure that - emotionally speaking - you are standing on solid ground and doing as well as you can with where you are at in your journey right now. Our goal here is to stabilize your emotions, to raise your emotional average, to raise your emotional maximum, and to give you the tools you'll need to stay out of negative cycles when they come up.

Our goal in this section is basically the microcosm of everything we are doing in this healing:

We are learning how to feel as good as possible as often as possible and how to pick ourselves up out of the low places as quickly as possible when they come around.

70

This involves a few things…

Feeling as good as possible as often as possible:

There are 2 main elements to how we start this.

The first is that we need to build proper habits; an overall physically and emotionally healthy lifestyle within the boundaries of where you are currently at. There are countless simple things that can be done, changed, added, or reduced in your regular daily routine that will help stabilize you emotionally as we head into the next phase.

Some of the ones I like to focus on with the clients in my course as much as possible are:

- Morning and evening routines (you probably don't realize how important the first 15-20 minutes of your day are in terms of setting your energy and mentality for the rest of the day).
- Brain food cleanse (also called the 'Social Media Cleanse', where we eliminate needless sources of fear and negativity in our lives).
- Ensuring a base amount of physical exercise, sunlight, water, healthy foods, etc…
- Getting comfortable with affirmations and gratitude exercises.
- Learning the myths, mistakes, and musts of meditation and just getting used to basic meditation (extremely important).
- Learning how to breathe correctly (most people have never even considered this).
- Mindfulness practices.
- And more…

These basic skills and easy changes will help you raise your 'emotional average' (the average level of how you feel on a day-to-day basis) and will help you stay calm and avoid dipping down into low energies when a challenge presents itself.

Picking yourself up from the darkness as quickly as possible

For this, we turn back to the intellect. The 'dark moments' will happen naturally when you're releasing old trauma (and just in life in general), and in those moments we will need to rely on our intellectual understanding of what is happening in order to keep us stable.

First, you'll need to remind yourself of all the lessons you learned already about what is really happening in a moment of emotional distress and how resistance to it is where the suffering really comes from. You'll need to remind yourself that feeling it, without resistance, is exactly how you heal. You'll need to remind yourself that it's all for the best. You will eventually even be able to appreciate moments of distress, knowing that they can't truly hurt you and that - by feeling them - you will get stronger and your life will get better.

Next, you need to start realizing and remembering the ways in which things are better than you think they are and the ways in which things have always kind of seemed to work out and get you to where you needed to be. This is certainly where some kind of spiritual faith comes in handy... but I had little to no 'faith' when I was pushed onto my own journey, so I try to teach things - as much as possible - in ways that require no faith in anything beyond ourselves at all.

So, one way we keep ourselves stable during emotional storms is by acknowledging the perfection of our lives and of our journeys. No... they were not what we wanted them to be most of the time and a lot of us have gone through some horrific traumas and had painful lives, but... if you're reading this book, it's because you are at place in your intellectual or emotional evolution where you are ready to move on from this pain, to heal and to become the best awakened version of yourself that the planet needs you to be, so that you can be of service to the world while enjoying all that this Earth has to offer.

The secret is that by the time you become that greatest version of yourself, you will be thankful for everything that got you to that point...

including all the pain, the struggles, and the trauma. You see... if you're not yet willing to believe that 'everything happens for a reason' from a universal perspective, then you can at least understand this:

When you choose to learn and grow from the bad things in life, then they WILL HAVE HAPPENED for a reason!

You create the reason for them to have happened by improving as a result of them. The moment that you change your perception of a past trauma from 'the thing that made you a victim' into 'the thing that made me the best and happiest version of myself by pushing me to heal wounds I didn't know I had', it instantly becomes a good - or at least acceptable - experience. When you let go of the pain of an experience and instead grow from it, it develops its purpose. You would not have become this greatest version of yourself if not for these tragedies. Therefore, the tragedies were actually a good thing. From a higher perspective, at least. (If that statement irks you right now, I understand... just stick with me for a moment).

Our ultimate best selves don't truly 'suffer' as the result of their lot in life one way or another. Without fear and without attachment there is nothing left to truly suffer from (except... of course... actual physical pain, but that's really not what we're talking about here). Whatever earthly traumas might need to happen along the way that might push us to finally become that best divine version of ourselves and finally live and die without fear, we will ultimately accept.

Most of the time, we were the ones who put ourselves into the situations that caused our pain. We made decisions that brought us into those relationships and scenarios in ways that could have been avoided. Think of it like your subconscious putting you into uncomfortable scenarios because it knows what your conscious brain doesn't - that there is a far better version of yourself and of your life that is trapped underneath your trauma and fear based defense mechanisms. Your subconscious is leading you into pain because it knows that that's how it can get you to uncover that greatest version of yourself that is waiting in the shadows. This is why - for example - you date the same type of loser again and again, or keep taking jobs you hate, or hang out with people who don't respect you and treat you right, etc... Your subconscious resonates with those situations because they have the same frequency as your unresolved pain and it feels comfortable there... but only until you confront your wounds.

You will be best off to start recognizing the ways in which encountering pain is actually for your benefit, as your subconscious tries to move you towards introspection and emotional healing. This has all been for your benefit! Things aren't happening TO you. They are happening FOR you!

***

Ok... Now... unfortunately, that reasoning does have some limitations when it comes to childhood trauma that we couldn't avoid, or instances of truly being victimized. People who have been kidnapped, enslaved, tortured or sex-trafficked, for example, would - for good reason - have trouble accepting this whole 'my tragedy pushed me to healing' kind of perspective. Some people really have gone through the worst of what this world has to offer, and it will always be impossible to 'make sense' of that stuff from within a human perspective. Please don't think that I'm making light of deeply traumatic events by saying that everything happens for you.

This is where a higher perspective of who we are at the soul level is needed to help us understand the worst traumas of the human experience. I won't dive into that here, though, because it would take us too far off track of the main topic. In order to make sense of the worst horrors of the human experience at all we would need to dive into a much deeper discussion of the metaphysics of energy and emotions and the collective evolution of humanity's consciousness towards our current awakenings – plus – the journey that your soul takes from lifetime to lifetime (for those of you ready to open up to that idea).

Please understand that when I refer to the positive elements of our trauma and how our subconscious created these scenarios, I am NOT talking about those 'worst of the worst' events of being victimized, but rather about the 99% of all other trauma that we have been perpetuating in our daily lives, and I'm talking about it from a soul-level perspective where the true goal of life is the evolution of our consciousness.

***

So, for those of us unwilling or unable to accept any of those 'spiritual' concepts that everything happens for a reason, we try to focus on how the bad things are actually happening to help us grow; on the things that we KNOW are good about our lives; or on the times that things have somehow turned out in our favor even when we thought they wouldn't. This is one of the ways that we train ourselves to pick ourselves up from the low energy places as quickly as possible.

We are reminding our conscious and cognitive minds that – in the past – the things that we thought were terrible weren't what we thought they were, and therefore, that this moment of suffering probably isn't as terrible as we think it is either. Additionally, we are conditioning ourselves to pay more attention to the good things in our lives, as opposed to the struggles and pain.

Gratitude for what you have and a recognition of the blessings you have just by living in a modern world and having access to clean food, water, technology, books, clothes and a roof over your head, etc... This is an important art, skill, and muscle that needs to be practiced and worked out regularly. Your life may not be what you want it to be right now, but it's – most likely – much better than you generally recognize during bouts of emotional distress.

Remember, you train your brain every minute of every day. If you train it for gratitude, you train it for happiness. Whereas if you train it to look at all that you don't have and all the horrible things you've experienced, you train it for fear, desire, attachment, expectation, and - ultimately - suffering. Pay close attention to how you are training your brain. If we want to be able to escape moments of emotional distress as quickly as possible, we need to start actively practicing gratitude for the little things, so that the brain can reset its default setting to 'gratitude and happiness' as opposed to 'fear, stress and worry'.

The fact that you're still alive and that you're here reading this book - that you're ready, willing and able to put in this inner work - means that you have in fact survived all of the things from your past - including the ones you never thought you could. You came out of it all, still strong enough to know that there is more to who you are and to want to find it. So, clearly... to at least SOME extent... everything really has always worked out for you in order to get you this far, ready to change and become the highest version of yourself.

Theoretically then, you WILL become the best version of yourself if you keep following this path that your trauma put you on, and when you get there you will be able to see even more clearly how everything really was working in your favor the whole time! You will see how your trauma provided you with the necessary pain that it took to get you out of your comfort zone and to learn to start healing. Without that pain, you would have stayed asleep throughout your life and never reached your full potential. From the soul level perspective, that would have been FAR worse than going through your struggles so that you could awaken.

Practice being grateful for how things are always working out to get you to where you belong, even when you don't see it or understand it and even when it's hard or painful. Practice noticing this pattern from your past and how things sometimes worked out in ways you never expected. Practice appreciating the things that make your life so much easier than it could be.

Just the fact that you live in a modern world where you have access to a book like this for the measly few dollars you spent on it is miraculous compared to what life was like a few hundred years ago. Or, maybe the way that this book found you at the exact time that you needed it can help remind you of some of the magic of this world. There is so much awesomeness about your life that you almost certainly never stop to truly appreciate while you're in the middle of your struggles. Your brain loves to default to reflecting on all the ways your life is NOT what you want it be, and that simply reinforces negative cycles that keep you from growing and evolving.

Acknowledging that is super powerful and when you can truly embody this knowledge that everything is always working to get you to where you need to be - that the universe is constantly conspiring in your favor - you will be able to start overcoming fear and the vast majority of all of your suffering.

Using this knowledge and other intellectual reminders as tools, we learn to stabilize ourselves during emotional storms and to pick ourselves up out of those low emotions and dark energies as quickly as possible.

It's important to note, though, the end of that phrase; 'as quickly as possible'.

This is because these tools, tricks and pieces of wisdom are only there to help us shorten the amount of time that we stay in low energy states, not to eliminate them altogether. To completely eliminate the moments of emotional discomfort - especially while going on this inner healing journey - is impossible and isn't actually the goal.

One of the biggest mistakes that we can make is to think that it's possible to force ourselves out of a low energy state. That's trying to control things again. That's resistance. That's fear. You are afraid to feel the uncomfortable emotions of that low energy state. That is the opposite of what we are doing here. You will need to learn that it is OK to be in a low energy state from time to time - to be in emotional or energetic distress. You don't need to fight it. In fact, so long as you don't resist it, THAT is where healing happens!

You don't get to release past trauma while sitting on cloud 9. You don't get to overcome a lifetime's worth of repressed emotions without feeling anything uncomfortable. Healing doesn't come by trying to force ourselves to feel good all the time. Healing will happen by ALLOWING the uncomfortable emotions inside of us to finally move, unrestricted, through us. Discomfort and suffering are not the same thing. When we can allow ourselves to feel some discomfort without adding fear and resistance to it, we won't suffer in the same way and we can finally start to heal.

So, our goal is to learn how to survive the emotional storms when they happen, and to be able to maintain enough awareness to remind ourselves that that is ALL they are... They're just emotional storms... and they WILL pass. All you need to do is hang on, relax, wait for it to end, and not get stuck in that low state any longer than you need to by searching for the reason that it's happening - thereby unintentionally creating one where there weren't any before.

Don't get sucked into the illusion of the brain that 'emotional discomfort' necessarily means that there must be an external problem that must be solved. That's simply not the case, and thinking that will keep you stuck in your low energies for longer than necessary. PLUS, it will prevent you from actually healing in those moments. Your fear and your need to solve a problem are what turn a potential moment of healing into a moment of resistance that keeps you in pain.

A state of discomfort is a natural thing that will pass quickly enough, like a storm, and a relaxed and self-assured response to that discomfort helps you heal by allowing your unresolved emotions to get processed through you. A fear-based reaction to that discomfort, on the other hand, is a self-perpetuating cycle that will keep you suffering for much longer, will prevent you from healing during that period, and will stockpile more pain on top of the initial unresolved pain that got triggered in that moment.

Get it?

The state of discomfort IS your opportunity to heal. You simply need to learn to release fear around it and to allow your emotional body to do what it needs to do, without letting your brain hijack the process by convincing you that there is some external problem that needs to be solved.

RAISING YOUR EMOTIONAL MAXIMUM:

You've been living in a fish bowl, and you have no clue!

Ok... that metaphor doesn't exactly work... but I enjoyed it.

You've been living with a glass ceiling on your emotions. You haven't realized that what you consider to be 'the happiest you can feel' right now is not even close to the truth of how awesome you can feel on a daily basis. You've been measuring your life based on a false set of standards derived from your 3D programming and trauma.

It's been so long since you've been in true alignment with the fullness of who you are that you have forgotten what true inner alignment, connection with yourself, others, and the universe can feel like. You've set up limits for yourself all over the place about what you think you can feel, what you think you can experience, and what you think you can achieve. There are all kinds of negative limiting beliefs that you have placed on yourself that you don't even realize are there and that you certainly don't realize that you have the power and the capacity to change.

It's been so long since you've felt some of these deep emotions that we are going to need to remind you about them and get you to actually PRACTICE feeling them.

It's a little like Peter Pan and his 'happy thought'.

In order to fly, Peter needed fairy dust AND his happy thought, because - as we know from just about any science fiction these days that incorporates magic or any kind of superpowers - it is actually the emotions behind our thoughts that give power to our actions. All superhero's powers are ultimately fueled or guided by their emotions. From Jedis in Star Wars to Mutants in X-Men and everything in between, we know that emotions fuel our power.

Point being... Peter Pan had to focus on a happy thought to fly... but it wasn't about the thought at all! It was about the emotion attached to that thought that gets triggered when he brings his happy thought to mind. The thought is just a way of accessing an emotion. More specifically, it's a way of him accessing a higher, more pleasurable, and more liberating feeling than he can generally feel without it.

BUT... the goal is to eventually be able to feel that feeling regardless of what thought we use or have at the moment, and regardless of what is happening in our lives. The goal is to stay in the vibration and frequency of 'inner contentment, self-assuredness and self love' even when we are facing challenges and unpleasant circumstances.

So... we need to help you find your 'happy thought'!

Of course... I don't mean that so literally. It's not the thoughts that we need and it's certainly not a single thought. We need to first help you connect to truly inspiring and positive emotions again, and then you will need to practice feeling them by actively focusing on the positive thoughts that evoke them and visualizing them for a few minutes every day. You are going to need to practice raising the bar of your emotional capacity so that you can train yourself to stay in high vibrations more often. We need to get your brain used to feeling AMAZING again and remind it that there is nothing wrong or shameful about loving ourselves, loving life and just being ridiculously happy.

RECAP: Step 1 is about building a proper emotional foundation so that you can be ready to continue with the healing process. Building this foundation will require an intellectual understanding of our emotions and our subconscious cycles, and it will require that we start developing some tools, habits, and techniques that will keep you feeling as good as possible as often as possible, and that will help pick you up out of the dark places as quickly as possible whenever you slip into them.

Step 1 is about providing emotional stability, raising your emotional average, and raising your emotional maximum.

Once you have these things in place, we can move on to step 2.

Step 2 - Breaking the Barriers and Healing Subconsciously

Now that you have a strong foundation and we know that you can remain emotionally stable under some slightly rougher weather than before, we know that you're ready to start confronting some uncomfortable emotions and start the healing, but the first step here is STILL not to dive into our wounds and traumas directly.

The first thing that you need to learn is what to do with uncomfortable emotions when they come up, and in order to do that we are going to need to bypass the mind and reconnect to our emotions directly. In other words, in step 1 you were building a solid footing from which to confront unresolved emotions, and in step 2 you are going to practice the skills of confronting unresolved emotions - before we actually begin doing so directly.

In order to safely and efficiently dissolve the unresolved emotions that come up in us every day, we are going to need to learn how to heal subconsciously.

The vast majority of the time, you don't actually need to know what you are healing in order to heal it. That is the true essence and beauty of *Feelings First Shadow Work*. As I've been saying this whole time, our healing is NOT an intellectual activity, it is an emotional one. Understanding is not what's going to help you release those trapped emotions. Going back to the sweat metaphor I used earlier in this book; our goal is not to remember and to focus on all of the things that should have made us sweat in the past. It is only to release that sweat that's trapped inside of us right now.

Our whole lives, we responded to our uncomfortable emotions by running from them and trying to solve the external problems, but now... with our new emotional foundation, we are learning to sit with our uncomfortable emotions without resisting them and without 'suffering' as a result of them in the same way.

You now know - at least intellectually - that there is nothing to fear, nothing to run from, nothing bad that can actually happen by allowing yourself to sit with and feel your emotions. This is what we have been learning and practicing in our intellectual overview and in step 1.

BUT...

Just sitting with our emotions isn't itself a solution! Sitting with them does not - on its own - allow them to completely release and dissolve, and if you just sit with them for too long without applying any true healing modality to them, then you will just get more depressed and worried because this whole 'sitting with your negative emotions' thing isn't getting you anywhere... and it's uncomfortable and unpleasant when you don't know what to do with these triggers and emotions. Then, you'll get more resistant to this healing process in general because you'll think that this stuff doesn't work. You'll develop more disbelief around the idea that you can ever truly feel better and that will get in the way of your healing. You'll end up giving up on healing and self-improvement altogether and just go back to sleep in your own life, playing the 3D game again until some horrible trauma shocks you back into awakening.

So, we are going to need to learn what to do to actually dissolve these negative feelings when they come up. In order to do this, I teach people techniques of, what I like to call, **Emotional Phase Reduction**. Don't let the name fool you. These are intuitive healing techniques that I was teaching way before I came up with that snazzy, academic and scientific sounding name. The techniques I use here are pieced together from various sources, then adapted and melded together through my own methods and experiences, but the explanation and the science of why this actually works (and the title 'Emotional Phase Reduction') comes from my background as a sound engineer.

There is a - kind of crazy strange and yet kind of intuitively obvious - phenomenon that happens with sound waves, called phase inversion/phase cancellation.

If you take a single sound wave, duplicate it, then invert the duplicate (if you flip it upside down), and then you play both sound waves at the same time through a single output... you will hear NOTHING! The two sound waves actually cancel each other out, because when the first one is at its peak (top), the other is at its trough (bottom), and those energies/frequencies are direct opposites of each other. So, when you run both of them through the same output at the same time, the sum of the energy being put out is null.

To put it simply... $5 + (-5) = 0$

One thing plus its opposite equals nothing.

That is what we are going to do with your emotions and your wounds. By learning how to connect to our emotions without running from them - actively focusing on what that emotion feels like inside of our body - while at the same time actively shooting neurons down positive pathways of self-acceptance, love and gratitude, we can apply the frequencies of those positive emotions to the frequencies of the negative ones, and allow the two to cancel each other out.

I know... its technical jargon and my words don't really mean much unless it works. But... good news... it works! I've taught this to enough people by now - people who have tried decades worth of other healing modalities, therapy, counseling, spiritual energy healings, etc... - and seen the miraculous transformations to know for certain that it works.

It's like there's 10,000 liters or so of trapped fear and pain inside of you, and every moment that we can focus on those feelings (without fear and suffering) while at the same time applying positive frequencies to our experience in that moment, we cancel out 1 liter's worth of pain. You are actively bringing up a positive frequency inside of you and applying it like a balm onto the negative frequencies that are already flowing, thereby cancelling out the negative frequencies. You allow one liter of past pain to move through you while simultaneously bringing up 1 liter of love, and the 2 energies nullify each other. Do this enough times and you will completely clear out and nullify all 10,000 liters of trauma.

No individual instance of doing this is going to show a marked difference in your life, but over time we slowly clear all of the unresolved emotions. One liter at a time, we dissolve the unresolved emotional trauma by applying feelings of love and gratitude to the parts of ourselves that are still in pain.

To put it more simply; whenever an unpleasant or uncomfortable emotion comes up, we can confront it without fear and apply the feeling of love to it. We - almost literally - pour love onto our fear and eliminate it. By running the positive and negative emotions at the same time, we slowly let the negative frequencies dissolve until they are all gone. It's a little like running hot and cold water at the same time so that the water coming out of the tap is of a balanced temperature.

It will take some time to fully release our bottled-up pain, but in the meantime it's ok because you're not suffering as much anymore anyway - because you're using these moments of discomfort as opportunities to heal, without fear. So, life is instantly better because you know what to do with uncomfortable emotions when they come up, and every single time they come up you get to deal with them and become a little healthier and stronger. Even your moments of emotional distress have become positive experiences, so there's nothing left to suffer from anymore! It's magical.

So, we need to learn how to allow the negative frequencies of our trauma and pain to move through us, without fear or resistance, while we simultaneously bring up the positive frequencies of love, trust, faith, gratitude, and compassion. By firing neurons down these contradictory pathways at the same time (fear and love) we can dissolve the repressed negative emotional frequencies and chemical memories that have been looping inside of us, and we don't need to know what trauma that pain was associated with in the first place. The cognitive brain is not involved in this process directly. It is not a logical or intellectual practice.

As an added benefit, by practicing these techniques before applying them in our day-to-day lives to actual moments of emotional distress, we will poke a hole in the dam that we've built up between our heads and our hearts and will get the emotions flowing again so that we can start this true healing. There's an invisible and unconscious barrier between your conscious mind and your deeper emotions that will be dissolved while we begin practicing these techniques – practicing 'Emotional Phase Reduction' will crack open our walls and force us to finally feel some repressed feelings again. By doing this, everything will start flowing again and we will have access to all of the buried emotions that we are now going to start turning our attention to.

This part of the process is often the most uncomfortable, but it's also very easy and completely safe - if you know what you're doing.

85

Self Love Exercise

In general, I can't go into great length in this book about all the tools and exercises that I teach people in my course. Partly because the book would just be way too long if I did and no-one would read it, and also partly because everything needs to be done in a proper order and it would be irresponsible of me to provide you with some of the deeper exercises without making sure that you've done all the prep work or are ready for it. Still, there is one exercise that I feel compelled to add in here that I teach people at this stage in the journey which is extremely powerful at breaking some of these barriers.

When you have some time and are ready to try to break through some blockages, find a mirror. Handheld or large, it's all fine. Look into the mirror and repeat the following phrase, "I love myself and I am beautiful".

Look into one eye and repeat the phrase twice. Then look into the other eye and repeat it twice. Then into both eyes, and repeat it twice. Keep doing this for anywhere from 5-10 minutes.

For most people, this is awkward, uncomfortable, or difficult at the beginning, and doing this is going to bring up some emotions. Maybe you'll start crying or just get choked up. Maybe you'll become afraid. Maybe you'll laugh. Maybe you'll just experience a lot of tension or resistance around saying these things earnestly to yourself.

Once these emotions come up, you need to allow them to happen. Let the emotions run through you and KEEP REPEATING THE PHRASE until these emotions subside. DO NOT STOP until you are fully in control of your words again, no matter how uncomfortable it is! Remember, you are safe. These emotions cannot hurt you. Allow yourself to feel them. By doing this, you will break through a barrier and allow it to subside and dissolve. The triggered emotion is some blockage in you that we just brought to the surface. We healed it and cracked it open without needing to know what that wound was about! No logic involved, just bringing up old emotions from the subconscious to be released by facing them without fear.

By the time you are in control of your words again, you will have opened up some locked off parts of your heart and brain and you'll be that much more whole, strong and ready for the next steps.

If you try this exercise and nothing happens, don't stress about it. Sometimes people don't experience anything for a bunch of reasons. Either you were just distracted in that moment and not truly connected to the experience, or your brain just wasn't in the right frequency at the time to connect to your reservoir of trapped emotion, or there is a delayed reaction that is going to happen and you might release the energy later, or - in some cases - you've already broken past your most basic boundaries and feel comfortable enough for this exercise already. In other cases, your brain is protecting you because you're genuinely not ready to feel what needs to be felt yet. Everything does happen in divine timing, as frustrating as that is to hear sometimes.

Whatever it is, whether you experience anything or not, by performing this (and a similar partner exercise) a few times you will practice connecting to your emotions, giving and receiving love to yourself, and healing wounds without needing to know what you are healing. This will help ensure that you are ready to safely move on to the next steps.

*Disclaimer - that is not the ONLY exercise that I teach clients before moving on to the next steps, and there is a lot of other learning and preparation that would have happened by this point. So, if you are using this book as a roadmap to direct your own self-guided healing, just be careful about jumping to the next section carelessly. If you want more in depth guidance to make sure you have all the tools you need, I suggest that you take my course.

Step 3 - Starting the Conscious healing

So far, we have provided you with a strong emotional footing and the basic tools for releasing trapped emotions inside of you (without needing to know what you're releasing), as well as tools for handling negative emotions in the moment without suffering as much because of them. We have helped you to feel as good as possible as often as possible and taught you how to handle and confront emotional distress when it comes up - healing subconsciously without rationalizing or analyzing exactly what pain you are releasing.

Now, all you need to do is start applying these methods to your uncomfortable emotions as they come up! SO SIMPLE!

You don't need to go chasing down your demons and hunting for the secret trauma behind all your pain. Instead, you just need to learn to be still in the moment, to enjoy the good times as much as possible and to not run away from the bad things, because you now understand that those 'bad things' (the uncomfortable emotions) are actually coming to the surface to help you heal and release them, and that they have no power to hurt you.

I like to tell people, be the flower... not the bee.

The bee is flying around all day long from flower to flower, expending a lot of energy and constantly searching for the next pod of nectar. That's you when you spend all day trying to find your past wounds, letting your mind fly all around through your past and through the external world trying to find the next thing to heal or protect you from. It's exhausting and unnecessary. The flower, on the other hand, doesn't have to move or to do anything in order to participate in this pollination process. It just waits, and the bee comes.

This is precisely how you should be approaching your healing. You don't need to chase down negative frequencies, uncomfortable emotions and past trauma in order to heal, because this stuff is presenting itself to you all the time! It's coming up on its own, in its own timing and in its own ways all the time. It comes up in the form of your uncomfortable emotions. Every instance of fear, doubt, guilt, shame, anxiety, etc... that comes up when you are not in literal danger is just a remnant and a manifestation of your past pain.

The emotional discomfort is a reflection of your past pain that is still rolling around inside you. It's very hard to find the logical source or origin point of the emotional pain, but it's very easy to connect with the emotional and sensory discomfort that you are having in the moment. Your discomfort is your entry point to the emotional trauma. Deal with the discomfort and you heal a whole slew of wounds that it is connected to without needing to intellectually understand it. That moment of discomfort is a projection of multiple past traumas that all carried similar emotional frequencies, and by confronting the discomfort that you feel RIGHT NOW directly, you will help to heal those past traumas, without needing to know which past traumas are involved.

So, in the moment that a negative emotion comes up, that is your opportunity to do some healing, and when you're in moments that you're feeling good there's no point in trying to force yourself to do any healing. The name of the game is 'Enjoy the good moments, and turn the bad moments into healing and growth'. You don't search for emotional pain; you just wait for it to present itself on its own, and handle it properly in a way that helps you heal when it does.

It's actually pretty simple when you think about it.

So, the next time something uncomfortable comes up... what's the real problem here?

There is no real problem! There is only an opportunity for more healing! There is an uncomfortable emotion. Sure. It is not the most pleasant of moments. Sure... but there is nothing to be afraid of! It's no worse than a stomach ache - just an uncomfortable sensation that is ultimately nothing to worry about. Not every stomach ache is a sign that there is something terribly wrong with you and that you are going to die. When you have a stomach ache you don't start freaking out that everything in your life is terrible and that you're never going to accomplish everything you ever wanted to... do you?

Of course not! Because it's just a stomach ache! It's just a temporary uncomfortable sensation that is going to go away and you know that. So, you can more or less just try to relax and survive the discomfort calmly until it passes. Freaking out is only going to make the whole experience that much more unpleasant. Allowing yourself to slip into anger, fear, jealousy, etc... is only going to lead you to feel worse in the moment while simultaneously pushing you to make decisions and react in ways that you will regret later on.

In order to do this conscious healing, we work from the top down, instead of from the bottom up - meaning that instead of going searching for the psychological roots to our surface emotional reactions, we are just going to focus on those surface emotional reactions directly, learn how to deal with them, and slowly follow the breadcrumb trail down to their roots in a natural way where you are never tackling more than you're ready to handle.

I like to say that it's a process of excavation rather than a process of drilling.

In traditional talk therapy, the goal is to seek out your core wounds and your past trauma, and by developing a conscious understanding of them you will attempt to reprogram your responses to the triggers that bring up that past pain in you. It is a process of drilling down into your subconscious to try and expose and collapse some nugget of truth from the past that will - by its collapse - have everything on top of it shift and make you whole again.

There are many reasons why this is ineffective, some that we have already touched on. Those core wounds are too heavy for you to deal with right now, for one thing, and they are buried under a lifetime's worth of other triggers and traumas, for another. Plus, it's just not helpful to spend our days actively shooting neurons down the old pathways of fear, doubt, guilt and shame, because - even though you're doing so in an effort to heal - you're really just helping to pave those pathways even deeper. It's actually counterproductive a lot of the time.

Instead, with *Feelings First Shadow Work*, we are simply going to focus on handling our emotions at the surface at any given moment, and - by doing so - we will develop the strength and skills to confront heavier and heavier emotions. We will slowly clear away all of the fear-based programming from the top down. We are building the shadow work muscle and starting to unravel all the defense mechanisms, starting with the smallest triggers first and/or whatever is presenting itself to us in the moment.

So, instead of always trying to find the reason behind your behavior, we are just going to learn how to zoom inwards, how to FEEL the uncomfortable emotion that is causing us to act a certain way, how to heal the emotion itself and then how to react differently in that moment. We can start with the simple things, like... if you're in line at the grocery store and someone in front of you is taking a really long time to pay and that's causing you frustration, then... awesome! Let's deal with that frustration right then and there.

You know that there's no 'real problem' that you need to worry about in that scenario and you know that the frustration that's coming up is actually a remnant of old pain that is trying to express itself through you. So, let's use this moment to make us better, stronger, happier, etc...

Let's connect to that feeling of frustration that's happening inside of you right now without trying to run from it or 'solve' it! You've never just stopped and allowed yourself to do that before. Stop running from the shadow for a minute and look at it! Let's notice how it can't hurt you and how resisting it is actually a defense mechanism to help you avoid being uncomfortable. Then, let's apply our Emotional Phase Reduction techniques to this feeling so that we can use this moment of emotional distress as an opportunity to heal. Then, let's learn to be grateful for having been triggered by this event because it gave you that opportunity to heal and grow, and now that you have confronted the emotion instead of running from it you are a little stronger, a little wiser, and a little more capable of handling even stronger negative emotions the next time they come up.

Your life is now better because this person in front of you brought up frustration inside of you in an instance where you knew that you were safe to feel it and heal it. You should thank this person!

In my experience and that of my clients, this 'excavation' process is not only simpler, but far more effective than the drilling process that traditional therapy likes to engage in. I mentioned earlier how your core wounds are like the 200-pound weights of emotional distress and that you are currently not strong enough to lift 5 pounds. That is precisely what the drilling process tries to do. Before giving you any tools or any foundation of what to do with negative emotions and your inner pain, they are going to dive into the worst wounds that happened, hoping that an intellectual understanding of this is going to create the shift in your brain that will eliminate your pain and bad behaviors. That is exactly like trying to lift 200 pounds on your first go at the gym. It's likely to lead to injury and to discouraging you about this whole 'working out' concept altogether.

It is much safer and more efficient to build the shadow work muscle naturally as you go, and to even experience the benefits of this work bit by bit as you progressively dive deeper into your triggers - instead of trying to jump right to the heaviest weights while you're still in your lowest emotional states. This can be a very natural and simple process! Let's practice enjoying life more and not suffering as much, by simply releasing our fears and resistance to things that can't actually hurt us. That's it. It's EASY!

Catch Some Waves!

I like to say that the healing process is akin to learning how to surf.

Before you went through any kind of 'awakening' or raising of your consciousness to the point where you could even notice these emotional cycles that you've been in, it was like you were underneath the surface of the water. You didn't really notice that there were waves going on. You were just swimming in the undertow, more or less oblivious to the true nature of the sea around you.

Now that you can see these cycles and observe your surroundings, it's like you're at the surface of the water sitting on your surfboard. You can notice the emotional waves and the movement of the ocean, and there's no going back down. You can't pretend you don't know and don't see this stuff once you know and see it. Your only option would be to pretend that it's not real and to ignore it, and that's just going to lead to more suffering.

I.e. - you can't go back under the sea. Sorry, Ariel.

So, now that you're on the surface, you're going to need to learn to ride bigger and bigger waves if you want to stay on your surfboard as often as possible (where 'on your board' is akin to 'emotionally stable, happy, and in control'). At the beginning, even riding a 2-foot wave is tricky. You might not get on the wave in the first place (you might not catch your emotional trigger before you react to it), you might not get up on your board if you do (you might not successfully interrupt your old programmed reaction), or you might get up and then fall off (you might try to change, but slip back into old habits). That is all to be expected.

But as you practice more and more on the 2-foot waves, that will become simple and second nature. Soon you'll be able to move on to the 5-foot waves.

That's how you will start handling the emotional distresses in your life. When one of the light triggers comes up, it won't even register to you anymore as a 'trigger'. When the medium sized ones come up, you won't be distracted. You'll just tighten up your form a bit and ride it with pleasure. When the super big waves come, you'll brace yourself and do what you can. Whenever you get knocked off your board, you'll remind yourself that that's ok, that there's absolutely nothing to worry about, and you'll wait for that set of big waves to pass, then get right back up on your board.

Eventually you'll get to the point where even the biggest waves can't knock you off your board anymore, and where you are - for all intents and purposes - emotionally invulnerable.

That is the goal. To become so strong at riding emotional waves that none of them can ever truly throw you too far off your board anymore. NOT to never experience emotional waves again. There will never be a time when you are not experiencing ups and downs in your life. It is the very nature of reality. Every day is followed by a night. Every crest is followed by a trough. Every hill, by a valley. One thing on its own cannot exist, and a thing that is not in movement does not live. There needs to be change and for there to be change, there need to be waves. But when you can learn to ride even the biggest waves skillfully, then you can remain calm and in control through any storm, and the storm doesn't seem so bad anymore. It just means that there are bigger waves to ride for a while. You can even learn to enjoy surfing them!

When you can achieve this (when you can learn to ride even the biggest waves without being tricked into perpetuating self-harming, fear-based cycles), every moment is more pleasant, and success in any area of your life becomes inevitable.

Got a minute?

Hey there!

Quick interruption. Are you enjoying this book? Are you finding it helpful? Do you believe that it can help others and that the ideas in this book are worth sharing?

Do you believe that the world would be a better place if more people understood the things that you are learning here and if more people dove into this healing?

If so, **please** take a minute right now and go leave a review for this book on Amazon or on GoodReads (or wherever else you might share your literary love). This will seriously go a long way to helping others know that there is valuable information here.

Once you've done that, please consider making a post about this book on social media. Help me spread the word!

Thank you so much for taking the time! It truly means a lot to me, and it will help spread these important lessons and push us collectively to a brighter world. You sharing this book with someone might be the very thing that turns their whole life around.

A digital copy of this book can be purchased at http://BenjyShererCoaching.com/ffbook. Physical copies and Kindle versions can be found on Amazon and some other online retailers. Audiobooks are also available.

Now, back to the book.

STAGE 2 - THE REPROGRAMMING

Step 4 – The Heart Space and Unconditional Love

Those first 3 steps are all part of 'stage 1' where we are focusing specifically on the direct 'healing'. We build the foundation, we break the barriers, and we start this top-down process of confronting our triggers, building our shadow work muscle, and undoing the layers of fear-based programing, bit by bit and naturally as we go.

While you continue to do this work from stage 1, we move on to stage 2; where we start working on actively building the new paradigm for yourself. While you work on undoing old programming, it is absolutely crucial that we start actively developing new programming. No amount of 'healing' on its own is going to fully get us out of these old cycles otherwise, because your brain has no alternate route to go down when it gets triggered enough to fall off the surfboard. If we don't begin to actively train new pathways and new responses to old triggers, then your old pathways will always be the most prominent and most natural path for your brain to take.

Water always flows to the lowest point, and that's all there is to it. Without building new roads, you will eventually slip back into your old habits. You've spent a lifetime walking down those old pathways, so until you start developing new ones and actively pushing yourself to pave them, the old ones will still be the path of least resistance and you will inevitably slip back into them.

The first step in stage 2 has to do with the heart space and unconditional love.

Now that we've been doing all of this inner work towards developing self love, it's time to start learning how to apply these growing muscles and skills to our lives and to our interactions with the outside world. If in stage 1 we were pulling back all of our energy so that we could reclaim ourselves and clean all that junk inside, then now we are learning how to put our new and purified energy back out into the world. We had to retreat to transform and turn ourselves inside out, and now we will learn how to interact with the world in a new, more enlightened, more compassionate, more unconditionally loving way so that we can maintain this new inner peace while we continue to live our lives.

4A - Connecting to the Heart Space

Now that we have broken the barrier between the head and the heart and we have been practicing feeling both our good emotions and our bad emotions more directly, it's time to learn how to shift out of our heads more often and to start truly living from our hearts. In stage 1, we re-opened access to our hearts and now it's time to learn how to live there.

And yes... I know... that's perhaps the most esoteric/spiritual thing I've said so far. The most 'woo-woo' or hippy sounding phrase of this book yet. What does it mean to "connect to the heart space" or "live from the heart"? That doesn't sound very 'scientific', Benjy!

What it means is to learn how to bypass your cognitive experience of reality for a moment and re-prioritize your emotional experience.

Or... in plain English... to learn how to stop thinking so much and to let your emotions guide you instead. Your heart and your brain speak different languages. More aptly, your heart doesn't work on 'language' at all. Your heart works on pure frequency - without words. We need to learn how to listen to frequency again and how to let it guide us, even when our conscious, language-based brain doesn't understand. Your heart is actually much more suited to guiding you through your life than your head ever was anyway, and learning to let your heart lead the way will allow you to experience an inner alignment that will put everything in your life into a positive spin while putting all of your problems into perspective.

It all starts with connecting to the heart space, and there are a few things that this will entail.

One element of this is learning how to consciously connect more with our bodies. How to be more aware of and present with the core of our physical selves. In western society, most people - if they were forced to point to a part of their body to identify where the 'you' that is you lives - would point to their heads. We see the intellect, our brain and our primary sense organs as paramount and we tend to feel as if our heads are where our consciousness is located.

In ancient eastern cultures - and likely still in some modern ones - people will more readily point to their hearts to answer that question.

We live very much up in our heads, but both at a physical and emotional level we need to reconnect our conscious awareness to the emotional, energetic, and physical sensations happening inside of us at any moment. We need to identify with the more innate, unconscious and non-cognitive parts of ourselves, and more with our entire bodies

99

and the fullness of our human experience. Our thoughts and cognitive awareness are just one aspect of who we are and we need to learn to more consciously be mindful of and embody the other aspects of ourselves.

This kind of body mindfulness will keep you in greater ease on a day-to-day basis by keeping you more grounded with your emotions in general, but also by helping to make you more astute about your body's reaction to all kinds of emotional and physical triggers. So far, we have been learning and practicing how to notice, observe, heal and release our triggers when they come up... but we've only been practicing identifying these triggers intellectually. Being able to notice these patterns more quickly, more reliably, and with greater insight by simply feeling them is absolutely essential to getting you through to the other side.

Identifying with your body and being more connected to it will help you identify and notice the uncomfortable emotions and cycles much more quickly than if we are constantly waiting for our cognitive mind to 'figure out' what is going on. Your brain has to see these patterns playing out and notice the consequences before it can act, but your heart can feel the uncomfortable frequency of an event before your brain can process it. Your heart knows immediately when something isn't right. You have the ability to connect with what these self-harming beliefs and patterns FEEL like, way before they ever reach your cognitive brain.

Every moment of emotional distress that we experience is pointing us in the direction of where we need healing. It's really SO simple. Whenever we don't feel good (emotionally) there is something getting triggered that we can heal. EVERY time! Except, of course, in those rare moments of legitimate danger.

We also need to start practicing listening to what our hearts actually do want. We have so far put all of our focus on listening to the buried pain that the heart had to share with us, and now it's time to start learning how to hear our hearts in a more positive sense as well. This is the foundation of true emotional freedom. When you can truly learn to follow what your heart is telling you without fear or doubt and without needing to understand why your heart wants that, you are free, and you get to act in true alignment with yourself - towards unconditional self love - all the time.

Now... don't go getting pedantic on me with all kinds of "what if my heart tells me to walk into traffic" sort of things... "you can't possibly mean that we should follow our hearts to our deaths!".

No... of course not. Obviously, if your whim is to do something that is obviously foolish, harmful, dangerous or wrong... DON'T DO IT... More importantly, though, if that's what you think your heart is leading you towards, that's NOT your heart talking, and you simply haven't learned how to distinguish between fear and love yet. I wouldn't - for example - give the advice of 'just follow your heart' to a crack addict, because that person still has a lot of demons to work through before they would be capable of connecting to their hearts and learning to hear it in the way that you will be by the time you've reached this point in your healing journey. I assure you; your heart ALWAYS knows what's best and is always leading you in the right direction. No exceptions. You just need to learn how to hear it, and to practice hearing it and distinguishing it from fear or logic first. It's a skill.

As for 'why can you trust your heart to guide you?'

Well, firstly... as we were saying earlier, the whole goal here is to get our 3 brains into alignment because that's how we can find inner peace, and since we can't force our hearts to want or not want anything but the cognitive brain CAN be programmed, our **only** real option is to get our cognitive brain in line with our hearts' desires. Nothing else will do! Any action or decision that contradicts the will of the heart necessarily causes conflict inside of us - which will then cause other problems in our lives and more pain for ourselves and others. So, for that reason alone we should always choose to follow the heart.

But also, the heart actually produces an electro-magnetic field that extends 3-5 feet in every direction and carries with it our energetic signature and a lot of information that our cognitive brain is completely unaware of. Intuitive - non language based - information. Everyone around us, the Earth itself, and all manner of organic material (as well as electrical devices and even inorganic objects) are constantly emitting their own electro-magnetic fields as well, carrying and emitting their own energetic signatures and unconscious information.

When the electromagnetic fields of our hearts interact with the electromagnetic fields of other people (or anything else) they exchange energy and information. Our hearts are actually much more tapped into the energy and flow of the world around us than our heads are, and the more that we learn to listen to them, the better. The heart doesn't express this in 'language', it expresses it to us through emotions and other 'energetic sensations', and the more that you learn to speak that language the more that you will realize how much your heart has been trying to tell you this whole time.

It is literally true that you can feel another person's energy when you are close enough to them. Most of us are just too distracted in our lives and too disconnected from our emotions to notice this and to practice it, but it is a 'sixth sense' that every human has. It's just very subtle most of the time compared to the bigger signals and messages you're constantly being bombarded with from the outside world, and you've never been taught how to focus in and pay attention to it.

There are far too many denser energies and sensations drawing our attention all the time. Those messages from the heart have been a tiny voice in a big crowd trying to get our attention, and we have to train ourselves to be sensitive enough to notice those subtle signals our hearts are sending us. The walls that we've built up around our pain prevent us from feeling these signals, but when we can learn to consciously feel and notice them, we can start adapting our behavior to what our hearts are telling us to do, based on unconscious information that our brains can't make sense of.

I mean... obviously there are limits to how this works and we still need to apply reason once we have decided to listen to our hearts, but that doesn't make this any less real. For example, I wouldn't suggest that you sit down with a list of stocks and pick which one to invest in based on what your heart feels about their names. That's not how this works, but your heart is always talking to you and it will always guide you in the right direction, if you just learn to listen to it properly.

The Heart Radar

This is a fun exercise I give to my clients to help them build this connection to their hearts and to learn to trust and follow their feelings, and it can help you make decisions when you're stuck on something. It occurs to me that this exercise should really be called the 'Heart Lie Detector' or 'Heart Polygraph', but hey.... 'Heart Radar' just sounds better.

The way that this works is that you are basically going to be using your inner energetic sensations as a lie detector to determine whether or not to move forward with a particular decision. More importantly though, this exercise will teach you how to start bypassing your brain and connecting to your heart - using feelings (instead of language and logic) to guide you.

The first thing that you are going to need to do is to calm yourself. Best done by 2-10 minutes of meditation or yoga or deep breathing (depending on your experience level with meditation and mindfulness). Allow your mind the space to settle down a little bit. You need to allow it time to switch frequencies from 'active, real world, hustle and bustle problem solving' to 'relaxation and awareness'. The same way that your brain changes frequencies between sleeping and waking states, it switches between various other states in relation to our emotions, awareness, and conscious lucidity. So, first allow some time for your mind to settle down.

Then, you will start by focusing on your heart space. The literal physical place where your heart is... but a little more centered. The center of the core of your being. Shift your focus to that area and feel it. You can visualize bringing light into that area if you want, or picture the energy moving in a circle, or just try to feel that part of yourself. Place your hands over your heart to help with this, if you'd like.

Next, start by making statements where you know that a positive feeling is attached to them. For example, make a statement about someone you truly love and see what that feels like in your heart space. Make a statement about something you're passionate about and see what that feels like. Make a statement about something you accomplished that you're proud of or some good deed you did that made you feel good. Make these statements and see what they feel like. These are your test questions to see what a 'yes' or 'good choice' feels like.

Then shift to testing your 'no' response. Tell a lie and see what that feels like. Make a statement about something you hate, or a statement about a difficult and painful time in your life, etc... make statements that you know are associated with a negative response and see what they feel like in your heart.

So, now you know what a good response feels like and what a bad response feels like.

Then, make a statement about something you are trying to make a decision about. Make the statement as if you have already decided about it in a given direction and see how that statement feels compared to your test statements. If it feels like the good ones did, then it's what your heart is telling you to do. If it feels bad then it's not in alignment with what your heart wants, and as you already know - going against your heart is going to cause internal conflict no matter what outcome it leads to.

Simple as that! The challenge, of course, is learning to get your brain into alignment with a decision that it doesn't fully understand (how to allow yourself to follow the guidance of your heart when your brain can't make sense of why this is the best choice), but of course... that's really what we're working on overall, isn't it? Eliminating fear to allow ourselves to follow our feelings and be true to ourselves. That's the goal. That's where inner freedom comes from. We'll work on this a little more in step 6, but we're building the foundations now.

4B - Projecting Love Outwards

Now that we are more connected to our feelings and to our hearts, we need to learn how to project this unconditional self love onto the outside world. We need to learn how to act and react to others in such a way that our actions are always an extension of the self love that we feel for ourselves, and in a way that fuels our self love, instead of detracting from it.

Some people think that this sounds like I'm saying that you can be selfish and greedy and just do whatever you want to because your actions should be feeding SELF love, so just screw other people! That's not at all the case. Keep in mind that self love means paving the right pathways in your brain and cultivating the right emotions. It's not about instantaneous practical 3D pleasure and gratification. It's about inner alignment with the core of who you are, and at our cores we are empathic creatures. Being cruel, greedy, angry, and selfish actually cultivates anger and hatred and other uncomfortable nasty emotions inside of you that will continue to tear you up and make you suffer from the inside out.

So... no... as a matter of self love you CANNOT be cruel to others. You can't be slipping into anger all the time. You can't be selfish or judgmental. Those things go against self love. We are talking about TRUE, deep, soul level self love here. Not materialistic, fancy, 'I'm better than everyone else so gimme, gimme, gimme' kind of self love (which... of course... is not actually love at all).

We need to start applying the lessons we have been learning about ourselves to our relationships with other people and with the world around us. We need to learn how to be kind, patient, compassionate, and unconditionally loving to others in a way that this unconditional love that we give to them is not a betrayal of ourselves (in the 'overgiving' and 'martyr' kind of ways that we sometimes do). We need to learn how to have healthy boundaries, while at the same time being unshakingly compassionate for other people and their pain. This is certainly a tricky line to walk sometimes... but it's not really as complicated as you think.

Really what it means is that your own personal boundaries come first. Period! But when setting up these boundaries - for the sake of your own self love - you want to do so without dipping into anger, judgment, and aggression. Your desire to put up boundaries is well founded. Your aggressive and defensive emotional reaction, is not.

A few things you need to remind yourself of in every moment:

1: Any way in which others mistreat or attack you is actually a result of their own inner pain and trauma (because people who fully love themselves to the extent that you are learning to are kind, for exactly the reasons we were just talking about). When you see how much happier you are without all of the judgment, anger and fear weighing you down, you will start to have compassion for people who are still carrying those things inside of them and you will recognize their pain.

There's no sense in judging someone for being in pain, even if the ways that they are handling it and taking it out on others are misguided or 'wrong'. They're still just instinctively reacting to pain.

2: The ways in which their bad behavior actually hurts you emotionally is fully within your control - since it is really a result of your own past traumas and current insecurities. The other person didn't actually hurt you; they merely triggered some pain that already exists inside of you. It is your unresolved emotions and insecurities that actually hurt you, and that's up to you to deal with.

"A clean conscience laughs at a false accusation". (Source unknown)

When you are certain of yourself, the false opinions of another don't bother you. That is also true of the ways in which others hurt us emotionally. When you fully love yourself, in all the deep ways that we are truly working towards here, then no-one else has the power to hurt you emotionally at all. No one can hurt you without your permission. It is only your insecurities that give them that ability. Only to the extent to which your own sense of self-worth is wrapped up in what other people think of you can the negative behavior of another truly cause you emotional pain.

So, turn your reflections back onto yourself - again and again. Instead of judging others for their actions, you can choose to feel compassion for their pain (as per reminder #1 above) and turn your attention to what got triggered inside of you instead, so that you can heal it. This is the invisible option that you've had all along! Either judge others or work on yourself. It has always been easier to judge others than to recognize your own shortcomings, but if you want inner peace and happiness - you are going to need to start choosing option 'B' again and again.

3: A negative emotional response just won't feel good or be productive. By this point in your healing, you simply shouldn't see the point or the need to resort to anger or judgment anymore, because you have started unraveling the false belief that it will actually benefit your life. You recognize that you're just getting triggered, and therefore that acting forcefully on the thing that triggered you (instead of working on what it is inside of you that got triggered) is only going to make your life more stressful and bring worse outcomes.

Responding to others through fear and anger goes against self love and is only going to make your mood, your life, and the situation worse.

By learning how to maintain healthy boundaries without resorting to anger and aggression you will not only progress on your inner healing journey and get better at riding larger emotional waves, but you will start to experience less mistreatment and better relationships, because you will have cut out as much toxic behavior as possible. You will calmly and lovingly create space between you and negative, angry, judgmental, and vicious behavior, and you will naturally start gravitating more towards new, higher consciousness relationships.

Don't worry though... you don't need to make any dramatic statements or cut anyone out of your life in any drastic ways. Like I said... you just put up healthy boundaries against behavior that isn't serving you, and you do it with compassion and kindness for the person, not judgment and anger. When you do this properly, you never have to actually make the direct decision of who stays in your life and who doesn't. When you put up a healthy boundary, you allow the other person to make a decision about which side of that boundary they want to be on.

If you - for example - express to a friend that a certain behavior of theirs makes you uncomfortable, you did the right, emotionally healthy and mature thing by expressing how you felt, and if you did so without judgment or anger - then you're good (ethically, emotionally and spiritually). Any person who 'deserves' to be your friend should respect a kindly expressed, genuine request to avoid hurtful behavior.

Now it's up to the other person to decide if they want to adjust their behavior or not. If not, then they are deciding that you are not worthy of their respect and - as a matter of self love - you'll need to walk away, but you gave the other person the opportunity first to decide which side of your healthy barrier they wanted to be on. You don't need to make drastic decisions, you just need to keep walking the road of self love, let good relationships gravitate towards you and let the bad ones drift away.

Obviously, this isn't a 'one shot' instantaneous thing when it comes to dealing with friends and family... Have conversations. Talk it out. Make sure everyone is on the same page and understands each other and make fully sure that you expressed yourself from calm self love, not from defensiveness or anger, and then... yes... if someone isn't respecting the healthy boundaries that you are putting up at this stage in your advanced emotional healing journey, it is completely within your rights, ethics and etiquette to politely and compassionately walk away - even from family.

If you do so properly, then it's not a huge deal either and the door is always open for a new version of that person - who has grown and is ready to treat you with the care, compassion and respect that you deserve - to come back into your life. The goal is to separate yourself from particular behavior, not necessarily from the particular shell of a person who performs that behavior. People can change... as you yourself are doing. So, the shell of that person can come back with a new energy and attitude later if they are meant to be in your life.

Like I said... you don't need to make a big dramatic statement from anger when you walk away from someone anymore. If you do, then you're not actually acting from self love in that moment... you're acting from anger, aggression and defensiveness. You're still just being triggered and not noticing it. You can walk away politely, calmly, compassionately and from a place of self love that leaves the doors of communication open for the future if this other person is ready to change. Sometimes, you just need a bit of space from certain people while you go through your own healing journey. Sometimes, you even need space from family, but the door is always open to reunite with them.

So, don't worry. The people who are meant to be in your life will follow you and the people who are not meant to be in your life will slip away. This will just happen naturally as a byproduct of you choosing to live your life through self love. The same way that if you were an alcoholic and you stop drinking, then a bunch of your alcoholic friends will probably slip out of your life because you don't want to be in the same places or do the same things anymore. If you force yourself to keep hanging around them, it will also be much harder for you to not drink. You can't hang around people who are negating the positive changes you are making within yourself.

It will often be the case that people who used to resonate with you won't anymore, because you are making positive changes that they are not. If they can't follow you into this new better version of yourself, you will need to let them go. Many of your former friends will (usually unknowingly and unintentionally) hold you down at their level because they don't want to lose you. They will encourage your bad behaviors that match their bad behaviors because they want you around. You are trauma bonded over this bad behavior and the negative emotions that fueled them. Your alcoholic friends, for example, will make excuses for you to drink. Don't fall for it. Rise anyway. Love them anyway... but walk away until they are ready to join you because you love yourself too much to stay stuck in those old patterns any longer. They'll join you in this new higher life if and when they are ready.

This goes for unrequited love or one-sided relationships also. I've been there... You eventually need to realize that if a person isn't treating you in a way that makes you happy, then what sense at all does it even make for you to want to be in that relationship? You don't get to take a person as a concept, in complete isolation from how they treat you. How they treat you is who they currently are, and you are going to need to let go of the idea of 'who they could be'. Recognize what they are and recognize that actively chasing and fawning over someone who mistreats you is in fact a form of self harm.

It's a normal and a common form of self harm, of course, so don't be down on yourself. Just recognize that it is indeed a form of self-betrayal and self-harm that you will need to put an end to. Recognize the self-betrayal and start realizing that this person that you think you want would actually just be a poisoned apple if you even got them. Recognize that you are basically aiming for pain and suffering by trying to be with someone who is bound to be unwilling and unable to give you the love that you know you deserve.

What do you think it means about your relationship with yourself to be chasing someone who hurts you?

I know that was a bit of a tangent... but I also know that some of you definitely needed to read that. It was a huge important lesson that I needed to learn. It is NOT the thing or the person that you are clinging on to that you actually want. It is actually just a feeling that you are pining over; a feeling that you once had when you were with them or that you think that they can give you (even though they are not giving you that feeling now). More importantly, that feeling that you crave from them needs to be coming from inside of you first, before being with anyone can be truly fulfilling and healthy anyway.

So... returning to the point... we need to learn how to treat others in such a way that all of our actions are an extension of the love that we feel for ourselves. Acting in this way will lead us to being unconditionally kind to others because doing anything less than that is a betrayal of our own self love. This is how we overcome the 'me vs you' duality of life and how we become the best version of ourselves to give the most that we can to this world. Prioritizing unconditional self love will fill your cup in a way that allows you to give more to others.

Self love is NOT selfish. It is absolutely necessary.

I'll say that one more time.

Self-love is NOT selfish! It is ABSOLUTELY NECESSARY AND FUNDAMENTAL!

We treat others with kindness and compassion because it is what is best for us at the soul/emotional level. That is unconditional self love at its peak; treating others as well as possible for our own emotional benefit, and walking away from them without judgment or anger when our love simply cannot overpower their pain.

Step 5 - Physical Reality

It wouldn't really do a huge amount of good for us to make all of these inner changes without also attending to our physical realities, would it?

Your inner world and outer world are in a constant state of 'co-creation'. Think of it like 'one hand draws the other'. The two are always playing back and forth at each other. It's kind of like a dance. Your thoughts and emotions lead to your actions, your actions affect the outer world, the outer world affects your thoughts and your emotions and so on... So, while you've been doing all of this work to raise the frequency of your inner world, you haven't yet put any real focus onto your physical reality to make sure that it can follow and support your inner progress.

Right now, your external reality is a reflection of who you are and who you have been, with all the bells and whistles. All of your habits, triggers, traumas and defense mechanisms are reflected in your physical environment and your physical body, and they are playing out old outdated programming, reinforcing it every day.

Let's talk about your environment for a moment. Most likely, you've never bothered to really pay much attention to this, but when I state it outright it's going to be pretty obvious.

What do you think would happen to any average well-developed child over the span of a year if you painted the words 'rotten child' over their bed, compared to an identical child you placed in a room that said "we love you" on their ceiling instead?

Is it not obvious that the first child would become accustomed to those words and develop patterns of inferiority, insecurity, fear and mistrust? This child would believe the words 'rotten child' at the core of their being without even needing to experience any other direct trauma. This would then make the child act out in a whole bunch of different ways - say... getting into fights at school, intentionally making messes, throwing fits and tantrums, etc... This behavior would lead to more emotional distress within themselves, as well as punishments that would reinforce the negative belief that caused this behavior in the first place. Feeling as if they are a 'rotten child' would cause them pain, the pain would make them act like a rotten child, which would then make them be treated as one, which would reinforce their belief that they are one, which would make them feel like one, and act like one, and get treated like one, etc...

This cycle would loop over and over and over, making the child's life continually worse in a downward spiral until this child was able to finally - like you are learning to do - notice these thought patterns and start taking control of them through shadow work (if they ever did at all).

The simplest things in your environment can have huge effects.

DO NOT FORGET... Every moment of every day you are programming your brain with what you allow into your reality and how you choose to respond to what comes into your reality. So far, you have been doing this passively, but now we are starting to look at these things so that we may be able to choose to respond differently.

This is not just about your thoughts. It's about your environment and your physical form as well.

Your physical environment - your home space, your work space, your car, etc... - is constantly programming you in more ways than you realize. The color of your walls, the state of cleanliness, the flow of air (and energy, if we're going to get into that), the paintings and posters you have up, etc... Everything you see and everything you experience is helping to program a certain sense of identity into you that is hard for you to escape from, especially when you don't realize that this is going on.

This is one reason why it's often difficult for people of one social class to truly and successfully migrate and integrate into another social class, by the way... Lottery winners who lose all their money. Athletes and 'flavor of the month' celebrities who get rich and then lose it all. People who just can't seem to break through their income barriers despite having all the skills and talent to. Much of the time this is because they have a 'poor man's mentality' that prevents them from taking those last steps needed to break through to the next level and this is often because they can't break through the programming of their current physical environments (this is partly where the advice of 'dress for the job you want, not the job you have comes from – internal self programing around a new identity).

Their surroundings and their physical embodiment are perpetually programming into them a self-identity that is not in alignment with the versions of themselves that they are trying to be, and so they subconsciously sabotage themselves all the time. If you don't see yourself as a wealthy person, it becomes hard to take the steps to actually becoming one, and it's hard to see yourself as a wealthy person when your surroundings are programming yourself to believe that you are not.[8]

I know this sounds a bit 'woo-woo' and hokey, but I assure you... take ANY of the great business and self development gurus and guides of our time - Tony Robbins, Grant Cardone, Dean Grazsiosi, or even Oprah and Eckhart Tolle - every one of them will tell you that the first things that you need to change to succeed are your own limiting beliefs and your mindset. They will tell you that nothing can be truly achieved until you have your beliefs and identity in full alignment with the goal that you are trying to achieve.

---

[8] For tips on how to accelerate the reprograming of your inner identity, see my other book *10 Mind Hacks for Quicker Emotional Healing*.

Tony Robbins likes to say, "It's not about achieving the goal... it's about becoming the person who CAN achieve the goal".

We need to make sure that your physical environment and reality is supporting you on your inner growth journey rather than continually dragging you down. Your environment and your relationship with your body needs to be such that - on your good days - you are not being held back by your physical reality, and - on your bad days - your environment and your physical embodiment are providing you with constant support and reassurance that 'this too shall pass'; that you are going to be completely fine and that you just need to wait this one out a bit.

Some of the things that you should consider on this end (that I go through with my clients), are:

- The importance of decluttering. (Everything carries old energy with it and keeps you rooted and stuck in the past. Many things we actually hold on to because of unresolved emotions attached to the time in our lives that those things represent).
- How you have your sleeping area set up.
- Designs and art in your home and work.
- Your diet.
- Your posture.
- Use of drugs and alcohol (I'm not saying that you can't use these things... I'm just saying that your relationship with them needs to be examined).
- Vision Boards and visual affirmations.
- Identifying toxic influences of all sorts in your physical environment.
- Importance of drinking high quality water.
- Importance of connection with nature.
- Importance of getting enough sun, and enough sleep.

etc...

These are all things in your physical day-to-day life that have a huge impact on your overall mental, emotional, and spiritual wellbeing that have most likely been sabotaging you for a long time now without you ever noticing. Even wearing the same 10 year old clothes that have worn out their use could sometimes be an indication of being unable to move on from a particular period in your life or from a particular version of who you are.

There are certain things that we cling on to as we get older because we are trying to hold on to our youths. Maybe it's a long haircut, a piece of jewelry, a fashion style, a particular item of clothing, an old car, etc... This is because our identity is rooted in those things. The identity that we are clinging on to was formed in relation to these physical objects and those periods in our lives, and our brain is still attached to the past, causing pain and suffering (yes... attachment is what causes suffering - see the second noble truth of Buddhism).

This identity that we have built up over the years - most ironically - is a fake identity that we developed through our defense mechanisms as a way to get along in the real world. The 'real you' is buried underneath all of the things you do to make people like you that go against what you TRULY want to be and express. This 'fake you' is your shield and armor. It is the image that you present to the world in order to receive approval in all the ways society has taught you are important, and it is out of fear of disapproval and rejection that you are clinging on to this fake you, not realizing that true happiness lies in letting down your shield and armor so that you can recognize that you are safe and free to live as your true self.

You're going to need to investigate all of your regular daily habits. How are you putting on this mask in your appearance, in your style, and through your home and decorations? How are you betraying yourself in order to fit in? How are you self-sabotaging by clinging on to the past or by keeping even subtle toxic influences around all the time? How is your physical reality playing its role in co-creating your inner world?

Be sure that as you progress through this inner journey, you adjust your physical reality as necessary.

You also need to pay attention to your body in several ways. The way that you breathe. The way that you stand and walk. The way that you speak. Even just the way that you hold yourself while you're sitting and lying down or any little ticks and nervous habits that you might have.

Your body is a singular organism, sending signals, blood, and nutrients, etc... back and forth and up and down between your head and your heart and your muscles and your organs, etc... All of those basic habits - like breathing and posture - affect the flow of these things within your body. A hunched over forward posture prevents blood from circulating properly and prevents your lungs from fully expanding when you breathe in. Not breathing fully means that you are not getting enough oxygen to your muscles and organs. Not getting enough oxygen means diminished functioning, which leads to problems in other areas (like mental and emotional health), and around and around we go...

The vast majority of people don't realize the immense amount of stress that they are carrying in their bodies at any given moment. In fact... check yourself right now.

Are your shoulders hunched up at all? Is your brow furrowed? Is your jaw clenched or your tongue pressed up against the roof of your mouth? Are you sucking in your gut at all? Or are you maybe just shaking your leg while you read this page as your unconscious mind desperately tries to release some energy that you're not comfortable sitting with?

I promise you, somewhere in your body you are holding on to more tension than you realize. This means that - in at least some context - your body is in 'fight or flight' mode constantly. You are not relaxed. You are in distress. Your body is signaling to you with this tension that it thinks that you are not safe.

These tensions that you hold in your body are the physical manifestations of the energetic and emotional remnants of past pain that never got released, and over time they can lead to greater and greater emotional and physical problems.

For anyone who knows anything about proper singing technique, you know that singing is about opening up. It's not about constricting your throat and tensing up your muscles to push harder and harder to get higher and stronger notes out. It's about relaxing all of your muscles and opening up your throat to allow air to pass through it smoothly and unrestricted, the same way that air moves through a French horn to produce sound. The more that you stress and tense up, the worse that your singing will be and the more that you will damage your voice. When you can open up your throat, on the other hand, huge, grand singing becomes effortless. It's NOT about pushing harder; it's about releasing tension so that you don't have to push at all.

This is a perfect analogy for what is going on in your body. All of the energy that is trying to move through you in order for you to be in tip top shape is being held back by the tension that you hold in your physical body. For those of you ready and willing to believe in the more spiritual conceptions of energy - you'll know that there's a lot more going on than just blood and nutrients flowing through you and that the flow of energy throughout your body is extremely important to be mindful of as well. Your physical body and your emotional body overlap in this way. You need to fully relax and align your physical body in order to allow emotions and energy to be processed and released through you.

***

On that note... for those of you still resistant to spiritual notions like 'energy', keep in mind that when I say this word, I mean it simply as a reference to the non-physical. There is more to us than our physical bodies and what our 5 main senses can actually detect. Your emotions - for example - are a non-physical part of your experience of reality that you know exist. Yes... you can point to the physical reflections of those things in your physical world (like dopamine or the firing of neurons down certain pathways)... but pointing to dopamine is not the same thing as pointing to happiness. Your emotions are real... even though you can't see them, touch them, or measure them, and there are other elements of 'you' that you can't see or touch either, but that are nonetheless real and that you experience consciously and directly.

Nikola Tesla - one of the greatest minds who ever lived but is not talked about nearly enough in schools - used to say: "If you want to understand the secrets of the universe, think in terms of energy, frequency, and vibration".

When you can begin to understand what he truly meant by that and how to start seeing things in terms of energy and frequency, you will gain a whole extra dimension of understanding to all the topics that we are discussing in this book. Think in terms of energy. Stop doing what you think is best for your practical reality right now if it goes against what is best energetically. When you take care of yourself at the energetic and emotional levels first, your life will enter a new positive spiral - and that's what we're working on here. It might not happen right away - because the old needs to crumble before you can start building the new, but I assure you... take good care of your 'spirit', and life will start leading you in a better direction.

***

To bring us back to the main point of this section, though... in order to take care of your soul... you will need to make sure that you take care of your body and your environment as well. Don't ignore the constant co-creation between your inner world and your outer world. Let's make the adjustments that we need to make to our bodies and to our environments, so that they can support us on this inner healing journey. Bad physical habits and maintaining a poor environment will hold you back from further growth.

Step 6 - Trusting Your Intuition and Staying in the 'Now' Moment

This is perhaps the most important and most rewarding step of the process, but it is also the hardest for most people. Fortunately, by working on everything we've discussed in this book so far - you will have been already training for this and you didn't even know it.

I think it's important to pick on that word 'training' here, for a moment.

A lot of teachers, gurus, spiritual guides, or just plain hippies love to tell you to just 'live in the moment', 'be present', and 'trust your intuition', but no-one actually explains to you how to do it! It's a skill and it CAN be learned... or, it actually would be more apt to say that it can be TRAINED.

Your intuition is a muscle that needs to be trained, exercised, worked out and tested on a daily basis so that you can deepen your connection to it. It speaks 'frequency' - the language of your heart - and you need to become fluent in this language. As I've mentioned already, your heart is always talking to you. It's just a matter of whether or not you have learned how to listen.

I watched a YouTube video once where someone was talking about how to contact your spirit guides. At the time, I was very far away from being ready to believe in the concept of spirit guides, but I was open enough to new information to understand that just because I don't fully believe what someone else believes doesn't mean that I can't take any wisdom from them. So, I watched the video, replacing the term 'spirit guides' for 'intuition' to allow me to absorb what she had to offer without getting bogged down in the semantics of the belief system they came from.[9]

---

[9] The idea that all different belief systems are ultimately different lenses for looking at the same truth is a huge, and perhaps essential topic that I simply don't have space to fully get into in a book like this. It is a much larger philosophical discussion that would take us too far off track from the central topic of healing,

In the video she said that your spirit guides are always trying to talk to you, but that whenever you doubt what they are telling you, you cut off the connection a little bit. Every time you ignore them, push them away and say that you don't believe in them or what they are telling you, you embed yourself more fully into the illusion of 'the matrix' and the physical reality around you, and so you become more disconnected to those other dimensions of yourself through which you can hear your spirit guides more clearly. You have to participate in the conversation actively (or at least actively accept and listen to their guidance), and if you don't then you'll lose your connection to them.

***

Now, even for these people who speak of 'hearing your spirit guides', the wise ones know that - in general - you don't actually hear some other voice in your head. That's not how it works. It just sounds like your own voice in your head, but it's the clarity and certainty with which the thoughts come through that let you know that this is coming from your spirit guides. It's about how these thoughts FEEL when they come through you. It's about the inner knowing that what this thought just expressed is in true alignment with who you are and the direction the universe is pushing you in. That's what most spiritual people mean when they talk about hearing their spirit guides. It's really just another word for what you would call intuition, but perhaps with a slightly stronger interpretation of divine purpose.

So... don't go overboard about calling these people nuts if you're not ready to believe the whole 'spirit guide' thing. Most of them are just talking about regular experiences through a spiritual lens. Don't be so resistant or judgmental against beliefs that you don't fully understand. Most of them don't think they have an imaginary friend by their side.

---

but it is something that you should consider; that all religions and all science are actually - ultimately - pointing at the same truth. They are all just using different languages and different lenses. They are all seeing different spectrums of the same core content, like if you used a camera to look at a room using either an x-ray lens, a gamma ray lens, an ultraviolet lens, a thermal detecting lens, etc.... You can look at the exact same object and see completely different things depending on what lens you are looking at it through, and all are equally true, piled on top of each other at the same time.

121

They are just looking at the world through a different lens and are more connected to their inner beings. Some do in fact see - or claim to see - spirits and other things. That's a whole different discussion, I'm just saying... keep an open mind to people who might want to speak to you in spiritual language.

***

This is how your intuition works then. It is constantly trying to speak to you. It has been speaking to you every moment of every day, all the time. It's just that your intuition doesn't speak to you with 'language' and the feelings with which it DOES speak to you are very subtle compared to the loud noise constantly coming at us from the outside world. The thoughts in your head that come from your intuition will sound just like any other thoughts, and it will be absolutely impossible for you to distinguish between your divine intuition and your conscious self if you are trying to do so based on the content of the words and the thoughts alone, or on the logic of the guidance.

Your intuition speaks to you through FEELING!!! And this is such a beautiful concept and revelation in a lot of ways.

Firstly, it means that - as I pointed out a moment ago - you have already been training yourself to trust your intuition this whole time! You have been practicing connecting to your emotions and your inner sensations. You have been practicing bypassing your thoughts and listening to what your heart has to say. You have been practicing acting in alignment with what your heart is saying and no longer betraying yourself. You have been practicing stepping over what you see in your external reality and focusing more on what's happening inside.

You are ready for this.

Secondly, it means that life is about to get SOOOOO much easier! You know why? Because once you have gotten to this point it means that you don't have to really think ever again! I mean... you don't have to plan everything out. You don't need to understand and rationalize every decision you make. You don't need to over-analyze every possible outcome to every possible scenario before making a move anymore. By the time you get to this point in your healing and you are ready to start listening to your intuition, it means that "if it feels right, it is right", and that's all you need to know.

Your heart is constantly pushing you in the right direction and all you need to do is stop denying it. Stop ignoring it. Stop saying you don't believe in fairies and just follow what your heart and gut are telling you to do, dag-nabit!!! It's more a matter of starting to allow than it is of forcing something new. You don't need to 'push harder' to trust your intuition... you actually just need to let go of fear, worry, stress and the need to overthink. It's about allowing your mind to relax when it doesn't fully know how things are going to turn out because it trusts your heart enough to let go.

Now, obviously... that is a big challenge. Getting out of your own way. Getting your logical mind to take a backseat to decisions that it doesn't fully understand and to allow yourself to TRUST your intuition enough to make these moves, even when your conscious mind isn't quite clear on how it is all going to work out is very difficult at the beginning.

Let's stop and actually investigate the word 'trust' here, for a moment. What does it mean to trust someone?

Without getting into a dictionary definition... it means to fully believe that this person has your best interests at heart and has the capacity and the ability to ensure that you are safe in their guidance, direction and care. It means being willing and able to let them take control even when you are unsure. It means allowing yourself to fall asleep in the passenger seat while this person drives on a dangerous road in the middle of the night because you know that when you are with that person, no harm can befall you.

That is trust. That is love. That is faith. And that is the relationship that you need to develop with your intuition (aka your heart, aka your emotional instincts).

How, then, do we build this trust?

Well, in the same way that we build any other muscle or relationship... bit by bit with work and practice, starting from the small stuff and building our way up. You will need to practice with the small things and meaningless decisions before you can move up to letting your intuition guide you on big decisions.[10]

Start by allowing yourself to follow your whim and fancy with things like: What do I want to eat for dinner? Should I turn left or turn right on my walk? Do I want to go out tonight or stay in? Use the Heart Radar exercise and start practicing this skill.

Practice doing what feels right in meaningless situations where you know thath the outcome is irrelevant, and practice noticing how acting in alignment to what your heart wanted just felt better. In and of itself, that decision felt better and you feel better in this moment because of it, and because you feel better you will act and perform better in the moment and you will slowly build more trust with your inner feelings, as well as steer yourself towards a more authentic life.

It is important to realize that the main reason that we want to follow our intuition is because doing so is - in and of itself - a better decision, regardless of the outcome. Going against your intuition and what your heart is telling you will always cause inner conflict. Inner conflict will then breed resentment, frustration, anxiety, etc... and those negative emotions will - in the long run - cause more pain and harm to yourself

---

[10] A lot of times, the opposite is true... but it's not what you think. Many of us have had times in our lives when our intuition has kicked in to help us make GIANT decisions even though we had not yet done any of this work or learned to trust it for the small things yet. These are grand moments when your higher self steps in. They are awesome. But if you have not learned how to trust your intuition on a regular basis, then it was just a fluke, and you still have to start with the little things to build these muscles properly.

and others. It's all a cycle that begins with whether or not you are acting in accordance with self love.

Remember that unconditional self love is the foundation, and constantly creating inner conflict by ignoring our hearts takes us away from unconditional self love. The greatest version of our world is the one where we tend to our emotional and spiritual wellbeing first and foremost because that will push us to take the best actions for the benefit of everyone. It's just that we all collectively have a lot of healing to do before we can get there, so there will be some ups and downs along the way.

It's a long game. Your intuition might not lead to the best outcome in absolutely every situation at the beginning, but overall it's moving you to the best and most complete version of yourself, which will - in the long run - lead to the best results for you and everyone else.

I assure you, once you have mastered this skill, trained the muscle of trusting your intuition and successfully steered your life in the direction that your intuition has been pointing you in, it WILL be the case that your intuition will consistently lead you to the best outcomes. Your heart knows way more than your head does and will always push you in the right direction. You just have to adjust to that lifestyle first. In the beginning, following your intuition might not lead to the outcomes that you wanted or expected, but that's only because your entire life has so far been aimed in the opposite direction of what your intuition wants. Once your inner GPS has recalculated to its new intuitive direction, however, your intuition will more reliably lead to the outcomes that you want in every situation.

The real beauty of learning to trust your intuition is that once you've built this muscle enough, you really don't need to plan anything or worry about the future anymore because you will know that in any given moment, your heart is there to guide you. If you don't know what to do in a situation yet, no worries! When the time is right, your intuition will tell you what to do. If you're worried about situations that may present themselves that you don't yet know about... don't stress... your heart will tell you what to do when you get there!

The more that you recognize that your head has no idea what it's doing and that you really can trust your heart to guide you, the more you'll recognize that you can't possibly plan things out or force things to happen the way that you want. Once you get to that level of trust and surrender, you get to just sit back, relax and enjoy life a whole lot more.

Now, that doesn't mean that you don't have to take action in your life and that everything is just going to lazily float to you without you putting in any effort. What it means is that when it is time to put in effort, you will KNOW it. Undoubtedly and without hesitation. You will have the will, energy and motivation to put that effort in naturally, without forcing it. Self love will push you to take action when the time is right. When you don't yet have the inspiration and don't know what moves to take, on the other hand, then it's simply not the right time yet. It just means that you don't have to - nor can you - try to force anything to happen. At all. Ever. It would be like trying to get off the highway in between exits. You can't! At least... not without killing yourself. You will just have to wait for the next off ramp, and until you get there you may as well just relax and enjoy the drive. Don't try and force any action until the next exit presents itself to you.

When you're acting from self love and truly tuned into your intuition, then you WILL take action when the time is right. So, when you don't have the right inspiration you don't have to stress about it and try to force an answer. You get to just relax and wait for the next wave of intuition to come. Life is SO easy!

Most likely, your life has already been going like this in some ways and you never noticed.

There have been plenty of times in my life when I wanted to complete some project. Write a book, record a song, film a video, create something, etc.... and no matter how hard I pushed I just couldn't get it done. I would get writer's block or just somehow get distracted or unmotivated, or I would work and rework something and never be happy with it, or I would kind of make something but not be pleased enough with it to release it, etc... These were moments where I was trying to force something that my head thought was a good idea, but that my heart wasn't truly into (even if I thought it was), or where it simply wasn't the right time.

Then, there were other times in my life where not even God himself could have stopped me from getting something done. Times when I didn't plan out what I wanted to do, but I just got so inspired, so motivated and so energized about it that I dove in head first. Before anyone could possibly convince me otherwise, I had already started, and before I could get anyone to believe in me or understand what I was doing, I had already completed it.

Those are the moments that you are waiting for. This book came to me in one of those moments. I didn't plan to write a book, it just started happening when I was ready for it.

Until those moments come to you, you don't need to try to force inspiration or stress to figure out the next steps. The best thing that you can do is just relax, stay calm, and enjoy life as best you can in the meantime so that you can be more aware and present to notice and take charge of the opportunities and moments of inspiration that will present themselves to you naturally and in perfect, divine timing.

Remember, we are trying to learn how to trust our intuition. So... if in moments that your intuition is quiet, you get antsy and start turning up the volume of your logical mind to fill the silence, you won't be able to hear your intuition when it gives you the next piece of life altering direction. If your radio is blasting, you won't hear your GPS when it's time to get off the highway. You need to be prepared to hear it, and in order for that to happen you need to be able to wait patiently for whatever is coming next. This is where faith comes in a little bit again - to be able to know that the next opportunity WILL present itself, and that if you miss that one there will be another, and another, and another...

There is always another wave of inspiration and another opportunity coming. Faith in this helps us release fear and helps us to be more present in the moment and to live more peacefully.

It's not even really faith, though! Not at all. It's really just observation. Is it 'faith' to know that even when the ocean is quiet, that there will be waves again soon? No! We notice patterns and behaviors in the way the ocean operates, and we know about high tide and low tide and how the ocean works. When it is quiet, we know that another set of waves is on its way in due time. Similarly, we are noticing that there are always more waves of intuition happening at intervals throughout our lives that we can't control. The only real question is, when the next wave comes... will you be ready to ride it or will you be too tired from all the paddling you were needlessly doing when there weren't any waves, because you were trying to force something to happen when it wasn't the right time for it?

Every once in a while, your intuition is going to send you the next big idea! Guaranteed. Every few weeks or months it is going to speak up and say "Hey! It's time for the next big step! The bus is coming right now! Get on!" If you're so distracted in your cognitive brain trying to play the old 3D game and to force the world into submission to be what you want it to be, you won't hear your intuition when it speaks and you'll miss the bus. So, you can spend your life in that stress mode, trying to force the world to be what you want it to be and to try to achieve all of your success through 16-hour work days and ulcers, or you can learn to relax and enjoy life and follow those grand moment of divine inspiration when they come, following the path of least resistance to your highest goals.

The other benefit of learning to trust our intuition and stay in the now moment is that we get to let go of things like shame and guilt - which are all about outdated memories from the past and the unresolved emotions attached to them. We also let go of worry and stress - which are all about imagined versions of the future that don't exist and are no more likely than all the truly positive versions of the future that could come to be. But, your head just LOVES to play the game of 'what should I worry about today?' That is how your brain stays in control. By constantly imagining the next possible predator and danger in your life so that it can try to plan ways to avoid them.

Your brain hardly ever tells you about all of the amazing ways that things could turn out. That's your heart's job... but you haven't been listening.

QUICK REVIEW

These first 6 steps are the core practices and concepts that should give you the majority of your emotional mastery; to keep you stable, strong, and putting up healthy boundaries while fully expressing yourself and living your truest life. The next 2 that I'm going to share with you are to help put us over the top and to truly make sure that we have nothing to fear ever again.

Before turning to those last 2 though, let's do a quick review of why - if you accomplish, practice and master everything from these first 6 steps - you should by now basically be in a whole new world of emotional wellness where practically nothing can throw you off your board anymore. I'd like you to imagine, as we do a short recap, what living like this would feel like. How free you would be. How anxiety, fear, codependency and more would be things of the past!

Let's start at the top.

It used to be the case that when something 'bad' would happen to you in your life, you saw yourself as the victim of this occurrence. The world was constantly acting upon you and you desperately had to fight against it and exert your own will and force to try to beat reality into submission of what you wanted it to be. You saw yourself as separate from the world and you saw your uncomfortable emotions as justifiable and legitimate reactions to things that didn't go your way or things that hurt you. All of these elements of your reality - your thoughts, your emotions, your sensations, and your actual circumstances - were all separate things that you needed to juggle and control.

So, whenever something would happen, it would hit your conscious awareness. From there it would trigger an emotional reaction. The emotional reaction would trigger discomfort (because it was bringing up pain from your past), and your response to all of this was to shift into your brain and into 'problem solving mode' about that thing that triggered the emotion, hoping that if you resolved the triggering event, thath the emotion would disappear and your suffering would dissipate.

This was a futile effort, because not only does solving the trigger NOT get rid of the true source of your suffering (fear and unresolved emotions), but another trigger is just waiting around the corner. And another. And another. And another. Millions of them. For the rest of your life.

What we have been learning to do with the *Feelings First* model is to approach this problem-solving process in the complete opposite way. Instead of working to resolve the triggering event, we are going USE the event as an opportunity to heal! The trigger is pointing us in the direction of where we need healing. You know how we know that for certain? Because if you didn't still need healing around this, then IT WOULDN'T TRIGGER YOU!

It's just that simple. Your emotional pain and suffering is within your control. So, when you are suffering, you can either try to eliminate the external cause of your suffering... or eliminate the internal one. When you eliminate the internal one, the external one doesn't bother you in the same way anymore and you will be that much stronger, calmer and more capable of dealing with the external problem in a safe and healthy way that can lead to better outcomes.

The first step then, is to intellectually point out all of this stuff to ourselves. We need to realize the truth of our own role in our suffering. We need to intellectually acknowledge for a moment that the external 'problem' is not a real problem, that everything is ok, that it is our emotions that are the real issue here, and that we can deal with our emotions independently from the things that trigger them.

Now that we realize this, we can pause for a moment and focus on the real problem... the internal emotional, physical, and energetic discomfort. We turn our attention to what is happening inside. Immediately, by doing this, we have already interrupted the old thought patterns and created the space for change and healing to begin. Then, we learn how to focus on those internal feelings directly and how to apply various healing techniques to that emotion, allowing us to finally start releasing it.

Already, there is no need to run from your emotions anymore. There is no need to worry and to stress about anything because you know exactly what to do with negative feelings when they come up and you know that there is no danger. You're starting to learn that there's nothing that you can't handle and never any real 'problem' other than the emotions that are being triggered inside of you. You recognize the difference between true pain and emotional discomfort and you're learning how to handle discomfort without fear and resistance. All of the things that used to make you suffer are now just opportunities for healing. 'Suffering' is largely a thing of the past.

Next, we have developed a new way of approaching the world and our lives so that we can stop the self-betrayal - learning how to live from the heart space and how to treat others with as much love as possible because we love **ourselves** too much to do any less. This not only helps our internal self-awareness and esteem, but it creates positive cycles in our lives and in our minds that reinforce all of the positive lessons that we have been learning. Plus, it improves our relationships, our productivity, and our general enjoyment of life, etc...

At the same time, we developed a proper routine and adjusted our physical reality to support all of these changes, so that even when we slip up mentally or have a rough day, all of the right systems are in place to help us bounce back as quickly as possible, and until we do bounce back we are calm and patient in the knowledge that these ups and downs are just part of the game and that there is nothing to worry about. We remain confident and assured in moments of low energy that everything is perfectly fine.

Then we learned how to trust our inner guidance so that we don't really need to plan, analyze, or understand things as much anymore. We get to sit back and follow our hearts to wherever life is taking us. Again... that doesn't mean not taking action... it just means that we don't force things into existence and try to control anything. What is right for us will happen naturally, and what we have to force isn't right for us. It's simple. Life is so much easier than we have made it out to be.

When you put all that together, there shouldn't really be much that can shake you anymore...should there?

Whenever anything triggers you, you notice it quickly, have no fear about it because you know what it is and how to deal with it, and you apply the healing techniques to it - rejoicing in the fact that doing so is making you stronger and leading you to a better life - and you just keep acting in alignment with what feels right to you while you calmly and patiently wait for each next wave of intuition and inspiration to guide you in your life. The only real problems are your emotions and you have learned how to handle those emotions so that you no longer need to run from them. Now, from a calm and centered point of view you get to head towards a higher and better, love-based world while just waiting for the right guidance and inspiration to hit to take you there.

Life is easy.

I'd like you to take a moment and reflect on what life would feel like if you learned to master these skills. How much better would your relationships be? How much better would you feel every day? How many better actions would you take and better decisions would you make that would have your life getting better and better every day? How much more money would you make if you were that much calmer and more confident and self-assured in your career? How many more opportunities would come to you because of how you treat others? What in your life would change and improve if you lived this way, without fear, doubt, guilt, shame, or anxiety? What would that be worth to you, and what are you missing out on every day by not living like this?

Take a minute and truly visualize all this.

***

This seems like a good time to remind you that my 8 week course is designed to give you all of these skills. You COULD be living this way 8 weeks from now if you sign up today (or at least starting to). I promise you, every day spent before doing this healing is a wasted day compared to what's on the other side. Don't hesitate. Find the course at http://BenjyShererCoaching.com/ffcourse

***

With that review in mind, hopefully now you can see how there is nothing left to fear, worry, or suffer about anymore. You are free.

But... ok... I get it. None of us is Buddha or Jesus (nor are we trying to be) and we are likely to still get a little worried or a little scared sometimes at this stage in the journey. You've learned the skills and you're practicing them, but you're still a little susceptible to the shit life throws at you, and let's face it... life tends to throw some shit at you while you're going through this transformation because you're literally changing the course of your entire life. It's a bumpy road.

So, we need something to keep us steady in those times where it's hard to remember all of these lessons or to embody them. Where it's hard to know if everything is ever going to be alright, and where we just don't have the strength to keep fighting. That's where Step 7 comes into play.

STEP 7 - THE SCIENCE OF REAL MAGIC

I was raised Jewish and even had some level of faith in the whole thing when I was very young. I remember having conversations with God when I was a child. Well... one sided conversations... but you get the point. Some part of me knew and felt intuitively that there was some truth to the matter.

When I was around 11 or 12 though, I started reflecting on the fact that I only believed in Judaism because I was born Jewish. I recognized that in the grand scheme of things it was simply a matter of chance and circumstance that I was born Jewish and therefore that my whole religious belief system was circumstantial. I needed to investigate and learn more. I needed to see all of my options. (Not bad for a pre-teen, huh?)

That - along with other existential problems that started plaguing me by that age, like 'why is there something as opposed to nothing?' -

started me on my lifelong seeking journey and my pursuits in studying philosophy and world religions. Throughout my studies I steered more and more away from Judaism, more and more away from religion, and more and more away from spirituality and faith.

That last part, I now realize... was a mistake.

We have gotten religion and spirituality all bundled up together in a false equivalency. They're not at all the same things, and in many ways... they are hardly connected at all. Spirituality is about a full discovery of who we are as people and what our lives and this universe really are. It's about tapping into all parts of our experience of reality and noticing the connection that exists between all things. Religion, on the other hand, is a system built around spirituality, and any time a grand concept tries to get codified into a practical system, it necessarily loses the core of what it is, for the same reason that you can't program a robot to feel love. There are no words... no programming language... no tangible set of rules or codes that you can string together to truly express and embody grand concepts like love, justice or faith.

And there it is... the word that was cringe-worthy to me for most of my life, but which is the essential next principle that we need to be able to embody in order to push us over the edge of 'never worrying ever again' and into the complete sense of inner peace that we seek:

FAITH!

That is the last piece of the puzzle that we need to have to make sure that we NEVER fall too deeply into fear or despair again.

Fortunately, I don't even mean faith in 'God' or in the 'Universe' or anything like that necessarily (although it's fully ok if that's your interpretation), but rather just faith in a conception of the universe in which there is more than just the physical. Faith in things that we cannot see or provide quantitative measurements of, but that we feel, experience and know intuitively nonetheless. Faith enough to believe things that sound crazy, but actually make a whole lot of sense through quantum mechanics, higher dimensions, or just plain self-observation.

We need faith simply in the way that I described above in regards to intuition. Is it 'faith' to believe that another wave of intuition and inspiration will always come? Or is it just competent observation based on years' worth of living as a human being and analyzing your own experiences? We only need enough faith to believe in things that we can't PROVE... like the next wave of upcoming intuition... because they relate to our internal experiences that can't be expressed or shown to others. Faith enough to trust that your inner experiences are worthy of basing decisions on and that not everything needs to be quantifiably demonstrable to other people in order to be true.[11]

You have observed - time and time again - patterns of your own behavior, and just because you can't demonstrate that stuff to other people doesn't mean that those observations are untrue and unreliable. They're not! But since you can't **prove** that, it will require some level of 'faith' in your own powers of observation about your inner experiences.

Do you believe that you can muster that level of faith?

If you're like me, then as you go through your awakening you are being presented with all kinds of ideas that used to irk you, that you are now having to get used to. Starting with the simplest things like meditation and energy (if you meditated back in the 90's you were weird... now all the greatest CEOs meditate daily), moving all the way up to seeing auras and contacting your spirit guides, channeling and astral projection, etc... These concepts start seeping into our minds, but they still just seem completely insane and it bothers the rational and

---

[11] This is where science begins to fail us. Science cannot measure or quantify our inner experiences, and therefore is limited in what it can explain to us. Our inner experiences are real and tell us a lot about the universe that science cannot, simply because they can't be measured. Most people have never examined their inner experiences. Most people disregard their inner reality and wait for the scientific community to tell them that something is real, but if you apply the scientific method to your inner experiences (of which you can't provide 'data' to others simply because of the nature of 'inner experiences'), you will discover a lot about yourself and the universe.

logical sides of ourselves. These new concepts are in conflict with our old belief system and it's frustrating.

That's a problem though, because only a true understanding and acceptance of these higher dimensional spiritual concepts will truly free us from worry, fear, doubt, guilt, and shame to the highest degrees. Understanding and accepting a higher perspective of reality is what allows us to start really living our lives more like a game and enjoying every moment. This is really hard though, when our entire conception of the universe contradicts these sorts of things... and it's not like we can just choose to stop believing everything we know about physics and our current view of reality (nor should we, of course).

It's true that - on this emotional and spiritual awakening journey - we start to learn that a lot of things that we used to think were true are actually false. A lot of things about society that weren't right, a lot of things about the universe and religion that were mistaken, and mostly a lot of things about ourselves, our emotions, our limiting beliefs, etc... On all of those topics there is room to budge and to discard old beliefs to accept a new reality. There is NOT so much room to budge, however, in other areas like physics. You're still human after all. You still live in a physical body. You still live in a physical world with certain physical rules and laws, and it would be foolish and insane to start completely ignoring those rules just because you awakened to some new level of spirituality.

It's one thing to believe in spirituality and to have faith... it is another thing completely to deny science. Point being, until we can make these two versions of reality - science and spirit - make sense together with one another, there will always be a sense of conflict in us which is just another form of betraying ourselves. So long as we see science and the new levels of our spirituality as contradictory, one part of us will always be at odds with another and we will never be at peace. Your brain will try to make you follow the route of science and your heart will try to make you follow the route of spirit, and the two will always be at war.

The ability to maintain faith in these more 'spiritual' elements of ourselves when times get tough is the last piece of the puzzle to completely overcoming fear, and in order for a modern educated person to achieve this kind of faith without just breeding a whole mess of inner conflict, self doubt, and confusion, they are going to need to be able to understand what it is that we have faith in through the lens of science, so that we can train our brains to follow our hearts even when doing so apparently contradicts our more 3D analytical beliefs.

Going back to Nikola Tesla; everything is energy, frequency and vibration, and you are going to need to learn how to truly start looking at the world that way. When you can understand the universe a little more as the multi-dimensional projection of energy that it is, then all sorts of weird spiritual concepts start making sense.

For example, we spoke earlier about how the heart creates an electro-magnetic field around your body that extends 3-5 feet in every direction. When I say it like that, it makes sense. It fits with your scientific ideology perfectly. You might not immediately believe it, but there is at least no contradiction with your scientifically formed beliefs about the universe.

Well, that electromagnetic field is what others would call your aura. Different words and ideology... but they are the same thing, and some people - whether you choose to believe it or not - can actually see auras. These electro-magnetic fields present themselves to some as color. This is not an overly rare phenomenon either. It's just that most people who experience it stopped talking about it a long time ago because people thought they were crazy, and many - over time - even lost the ability to see them, partly because they were actively pushing away the experience.

This is just one example of how even our sense organs are normally only picking up on a small percentage of what is actually happening all around us, and there are other dimensions and other layers of reality that our cognitive, restricted, and limited 3D human brains and sense organs can't detect or understand. There is so much more happening in the universe all around us in extra dimensions that are literally folded up on top of ours right now.

Let's try it this way: If no human EVER had ears or the capacity to hear, would we even know that sound exists? Would we be able to even IMAGINE what sound could be? Absolutely not. Even if we were somehow able to discover and measure soundwaves, we would never be able to conceive of what the experience of 'sound' was. We would be able to measure that some energy and vibrations are being produced, but 'sound' would still be a meaningless concept to us.

Point being - the human mind literally cannot conceive of or imagine a sensory experience of a completely brand-new type. If you never had vision, you could never understand what 'light' is. If you never had a mouth you could never understand what 'taste' is or what 'sweet' felt like. It's not possible.

So... of the 5 external senses we DO have, what on earth makes you think that those are the ONLY senses possible? Do you really believe that humans got the sense organs to detect absolutely everything that exists in this universe built right into our bodies? Honestly... it's just blatant ignorance and arrogance for us to think that we have true access to everything happening around us. Not to mention that we just know scientifically, in countless ways, that this isn't the case.

For example, right now - at this very moment - there are wifi and radio signals moving through the air all around you, carrying information that you can't see, hear, interact with or detect in any way with your body alone. You are oblivious to so much of the universe around you.

When you start to understand and accept this principle, you start to understand how things like 'spirit guides' actually make sense, how crystals can actually aid in the healing process, how you LITERALLY can bless your food and water to raise their vibrations, how incense can help enlighten us, and how reiki can have real and practical effects on our lives and on our health.

When you can begin accepting things like that, it opens you up to a new perspective about your life and the universe that should - if fully understood, practiced and embodied - free you from all remaining fear. You get to remember that this conscious and physical version of you is just a small portion of who you are, that this life is just part of a grander picture of the fullness of 'you', that you actually chose to come into this life, that you really are held, guided, and protected every step of the way, etc...

This is how you let go of those last bits of fear.

When you can understand these faith-based concepts in a way that truly aligns and coalesces with your scientific perspective of the world - you are free. You get to continue living and acting in the 3D world with the self-assurance that everything is always exactly as it's supposed to be - that not a single speck of dust in this universe is out of place - without ever feeling at odds within yourself. You get to continue playing the human game, knowing deep down that you are much more than human, and THAT... brings the magic!

There are 2 main things that helped me achieve this level of faith, where I now know - even when I don't see the answers - that I have nothing to fear anymore and that I can just wait for the answers to reveal themselves.

The first - as I've been mentioning - is an intellectual and scientific understanding of these spiritual concepts, based on the principle that everything is actually energy compressed into matter in different patterns and frequencies, creating the illusion of our reality. With my students, we go into depth about a bunch of these topics to express how the weird sounding 'woo-woo' stuff is actually fully scientifically legitimate, and that most people are just looking at things the wrong way or have been put off by language that makes it seem like we're out of our minds. 'Spiritual language' kept me from understanding these things for a long time too. Trust me. I get it.

The second element was simply being involved in this 'spiritual' or 'metaphysical' community for long enough to hear story after story after story of the 'supernatural'. It's hard to accept new truths the first time around. Nearly impossible, in fact. But after hearing 100, 1,000, or 10,000 stories, these things that seemed weird to you at the beginning start breaking through the barriers that you've put up against them.

How many people do you need to hear tell you that they can see auras before you start to open up to this concept? How many people need to tell you that they remember being on the 'other side' before they were born, or remember their past lives, before you stop being so belligerently resistant to it? Presuming, of course, that enough of the people telling you these things are clearly normal, sane, functioning and kind human beings, eventually you're going to have to start asking yourself some questions and opening up your mind.

The thing that finally put me over the edge was a book called *Psychic Warrior*, by David Morehouse. He was a military man who was recruited by the CIA for their remote viewing (psychic spy) program in the 80's. There was nothing overly special about this book per se. I was just ready to finally accept these truths, and hearing some of the most unbelievable stories be told in such a matter-of-fact way by the last kind of person you would ever expect to support these things finally pushed me over the edge. Especially because he too spoke about how impossible it was for him to accept and understand these new truths. Most of the book - in fact - is about his struggles getting used to this new reality. His family left him because he was struggling so much to make sense of the new higher dimensional reality he had gained access to.

144

I now know (or 'believe') 100% that Astral Projection and Remote Viewing are real, and that has made all the difference.

Even for those who manage to finally accept some of these concepts, though, not everyone is able to extrapolate from those independent pieces of information all of the amazing things that it means about our lives and the universe. If you know that astral projection is real and you are still afraid of death, for example, you haven't fully grasped this concept.

Do you understand what it means to KNOW that astral projection is real?!?!?!? It changes EVERYTHING! It means that it's true that our personality and our identity can exist outside of our body and outside of the dimensions of space and time. It means that you truly are a multi-dimensional spiritual being having a human experience right now and that nothing you thought was real, is ultimately real. It means that other spiritual concepts like law of attraction and manifesting are also (at least possibly) real. It means that extra-sensory perception is real... Basically, it means that you are actually an immortal soul playing a game on a planet right now, and that as soon as you heal and reconnect with this higher version of yourself and your higher consciousness, that you get to start playing with REAL MAGIC!

Life becomes brand new again! There is so much more to explore. You get to start living in an upgraded version of reality because you have upgraded your internal operating system to play the game with an added dimension of complexity. You get to start playing with energy, and there is no fear left to be found!

I highly encourage you to go and Google "CIA and the Gateway Experience". This will lead you to an article directly on the CIA website from the 80's that discusses what is known as the 'gateway experience' - a mental training protocol they would use to achieve a state of 'hemi-sync' (where both hemispheres of the brain are working in perfect unison) to help them achieve out of body states, remote viewing and even to communicate with beings of 'higher dimensions'.

Read enough articles and books like this, speak to enough people, open yourself up a little to the idea that these things might actually make sense scientifically in ways that you just didn't understand before, and your whole reality will start to change.

REMINDER

Quick interruption. Are you enjoying this book? Are you finding it helpful? Do you believe that it can help others and that the ideas in this book are worth sharing?

Do you believe that the world would be a better place if more people understood the things that you are learning here and if more people dove into this healing?

If so, **please** take a minute right now and go leave a review for this book on Amazon or on GoodReads. This will go a long way to helping others know that there is valuable information here.

Then, please consider making a post about this book on social media.

Thank you so much for taking the time! It truly means a lot to me and it will help spread these important lessons and push us collectively to a brighter world. You sharing this book with someone might be the very thing that turns their whole life around.

A digital copy of this book can be purchased at http://BenjyShererCoaching.com/ffbook. Physical copies and Kindle versions can be found on Amazon and some other online retailers. Audiobooks are also available.

Now, back to the book.

STEP 8 - THE LAST ANCHORS

That was the end of stage 2 (the reprogramming of the new paradigms - the new relationship between yourself, the world, the universe and other people) - and now we can finally move on to the last stage of this healing: dealing with whatever core wounds are left behind.

I don't have too much to say about this step in a book like this other than to point out that - hopefully - you now understand why we have saved the active confrontation of your core wounds until the very end. Why, even though this is what traditional therapy, hypnosis and other healing modalities are often aimed at right from the start, trying to tackle these things from the very beginning would have been a futile and truly painful struggle.

Only by now have you built a foundation strong enough to handle the load of confronting these wounds. Only by now have you built this shadow work muscle to be strong enough to lift these 200 pound weights of emotional distress. Only by now have you lifted and released all of the other weights of emotional distress that were piled on top of those core wounds, and only by now have you programmed your mind and heart with the new patterns and paradigms that it will safely shift into once we release these last anchors.

Without doing all of that first, we would not possibly be ready to or capable of finally dealing with these deepest traumas that we carry with us.

The methods that I use with my clients to achieve this involve self-hypnosis, childhood regression and past life regression.

**

It doesn't matter for the moment if you believe in past lives or not, by the way. I didn't believe in them when I did my first past life regression. I figured it was just a useful way of having my subconscious send me a message that I needed in order to heal and it was useful just from that perspective. As it was with all of my 'spiritual' beliefs, I only allowed myself to experiment with them because I was able to make sense of them from within a scientific or psychological context first. I could see a practical benefit regardless of whether or not the spiritual element of it was true.

It was only because of how real that first past life regression turned out that I even started allowing myself to consider the reality of past lives seriously. Learning to accept these spiritual concepts was a slow process that took years... but you have to start somewhere.

**

Even in this last step of confronting our core traumas, however, our goal isn't actually to seek out trauma and pain specifically. As I've said, we just need to learn how to feel good and how to deal with all the things that come up naturally that don't make us feel good. We're not masochists seeking out pain. We are explorers, getting more and more ready to walk into the things that used to scare us - like... walking into the cave of your past and seeing what it has to offer. We're not seeking trauma specifically, we are just walking, unafraid, into unknown parts of ourselves; ready, willing, and able to handle whatever comes up because we have built the necessary muscles and skills to do so.

We used to be scared to put our logic aside for a moment and to do what our hearts told us what was right. We used to be scared to trust ourselves and to listen to ourselves. We used to be scared to connect to that deeper, inner, intuitive layer of who we were. We used to be scared to feel every last bit of what our heart wanted to show us. Not anymore, though!

Now, we are simply taking our fearlessness to the next level. We are going to use these self-hypnosis methods to help us learn to listen to the deepest voices buried inside of us and to let them express whatever it is that they need to express, because we're not afraid to listen anymore. You know that these things can't hurt you, so you're finally going to go befriend everything that is left inside.

By this point in the journey - especially because of step 7 - you should no longer be afraid to confront any unresolved emotions or repressed memories, and you should actually even be kind of excited to do it because you know that it can't possibly harm you and that the more that you heal and release - the more magical, spiritual and abundant your life will become. You should be at the point of "I can't wait to truly live without whatever baggage I'm holding on to and I'm not afraid of it at all, so let's do this!".

Once you have confronted and dealt with even just some of the deepest buried stuff, you will be so strong - emotionally and spiritually - that nothing will be able to mess with you ever again. You will have so much emotional mastery, so much unconditional love, so much faith in yourself, in the universe and in your journey, and so few unresolved emotions left in you, that you will be - for all intents and purposes - emotionally invulnerable and on a constantly upwards spiraling life path that is just going to keep getting better and better with nothing left to possibly hold you back.

It's truly beautiful here on the other side! Can't wait to have you here with me!

Don't delay. The sooner you dive into this healing, the sooner your life can start moving in the direction it should have been moving in this whole time, and the sooner that you will get to break out of your old cycles and paradigms and into a higher, more peaceful, more enjoyable, and far more fulfilling life.

I'm not one of those 'Law of Attraction' coaches trying to convince you that if you just focus on what you want that the universe will dump a boatload of unexplained cash at your door, but I can guarantee that if you master the skills that we have talked about, your life will begin improving each and every day, until you yourself can create the life that you want to. Nothing happens instantly, but the keys to your true life are in this healing. Whatever reasons you might think you have not to start this right away, those are the exact reasons you NEED to start this right away! All of your limiting beliefs. All of the things holding you back. All of the reasons you choose not to move forward in your life. THOSE are exactly the things we need to break through.

THE NEXT STEPS

I'm so honored that you have followed me through this book so far and are here putting in this work to heal and grow. I truly hope that this book has already provided plenty of paradigm shifting information for you that has helped you change your perspective, expand your consciousness and understanding of yourself and of the universe, and helped you jumpstart your healing.

I just wanted to take a minute to remind you that this book is just the overview and an intro to the real practices that can help you completely overcome fear, doubt, guilt, anxiety, PTSD and more! In this book I gave you the full 20,000 foot view and as much practical information as I possibly could, but if you're ready to start putting in the real practice and work, and not just the intellectual learning, then that's what my 8 Week Course is for.[12]

In that course we go through the 8 steps to Self Love and inner healing that I outlined in this book, in much greater detail and with full A-Z guidance about all the nitty gritty. Every step, every concept, and every exercise, perfectly mapped out and carefully curated to make it as simple, easy, and painless as possible. We turn inner healing into a very natural process where all that we truly need to do is to learn how to feel

---

[12] By the time you are reading this, I may have added a 9th week to the course.

as good as possible as often as possible and how to handle negative emotions when they come up in a way that allows us to heal and release them properly. We don't need to hunt down trauma. We don't need to focus on all of our past pain. We don't need to try and rationalize or understand everything at the cognitive level in order to release it.

We just need to learn how to feel again and how to stop resisting what's inside of us. What's inside of you can't hurt you, but running from it DOES hurt you. Every time. We just need to develop the strength and the skills to actually release the pain that is cycling around inside of us, so that it can finally be replaced by the love that we crave.

Every week of this course has 4+ hours' worth of content to give you not just an incredibly clear and detailed 'how to' and 'step by step guide' to your healing, but also to give you a super deep understanding of WHY we are doing what we are doing, how it all works, how it all fits together, etc... The goal is that - by the end of these 8 weeks - you will no longer be reliant on me or ANYONE ELSE ever to complete your healing and to stay emotionally strong and stable, even in the worst emotional storms that you will sail through. It is designed to guide you to completely releasing yourself from fear and worry because - if nothing else - you have faith in yourself and the necessary skills and knowledge to survive whatever the world throws at you.

This course has been a life changer for all of my clients. I can honestly say that I have not seen a single person who TRULY just followed through with the program - even at the most basic level - and did not see some tangible results in their lives. If you just relax and commit, you WILL see progress. It is impossible not to, the same way that if you work out 4 times a week and stick to a healthy diet it is IMPOSSIBLE for you to not lose weight and gain muscle. It's just the only possible outcome to putting in the work - when it's done right.

Obviously, everyone's results are different and you do need to put in the work, but everything you need is there and it's not as difficult as you think when you know how to do it properly. The most difficult part is in relaxing enough to open yourself up to the journey. That... and trying to figure out how to do this in the first place.

After we finish the journaling portion of this book, you'll be able to read some of my favorite, truly heartwarming testimonials from past clients to inspire and motivate you, but I'll include one below this section as well.

If you're still reading these words right now, then this book has resonated with you and that means that I can more or less guarantee that this course is right for you as well. You wouldn't have made it this far otherwise.

I hope to see you there!

Learn more at http://BenjyShererCoaching.com/ffcourse

***

"The most important relationship that you can have in this lifetime is the one that you have with yourself. By healing your wounds, you not only heal yourself; you're also contributing to healing the world. Raising your vibe, raises our collective vibe. Unconditional love is paramount.

Resonating with all of the above is what prompted me to invest in myself and enroll in Benjy's course.

I cannot say enough wonderful things about both Benjy and the Course. It is immediately clear how much heart and time Benjy has put into his teachings. He is there for you throughout the entire process.

As for the course, it is extremely well structured with vast amounts of information. Each week Benjy provides you with a precise "To Do" list that assists you in truly embodying the lessons. So, whether you are someone who has been studying personal growth topics for years or are new to the subject, Benjy has you covered!

Upon completing the 8 weeks, I have already begun to notice changes within myself and changes in other's behavior towards me. More specifically I am feeling improvement in:

• Ease of decision making
• Non attachment to outcomes
• Relationships with family
• Making myself priority #1 without guilt
• Relationship with money

...Just to name a few!!

Barely a day goes by without another "aha moment"! The realization that our triggers are merely an opportunity to heal is life altering. It swoops you out of running from them and into embracing them as you would a friend. Changing our lens on all of the important matters that Benjy teaches, changes how you see EVERYTHING!

Doesn't get better than that!

Cheers to letting Love Rule and choosing to see our world from a higher perspective!

Much Love,

Danielle"

***

For those of you who are truly ready to experience these paradigm shifts in your life asap and don't want to hesitate, I would honestly advise that you skip the whole journaling process we're about to get into, and dive right into my course. As I said at the beginning of this book, journaling is just scratching the surface. For those of you who are ready, there's no need to delay. You can even go through the journaling process while you start the course, which will be incredibly effective!

For the rest of you, the following 21-day journaling challenge will help you reconnect to your feelings and break some barriers. It will provide you with an opportunity to start building those muscles and shifting out of your head. I have put a lot of thought and intention into making sure that these journal prompts can be powerful on all levels - emotionally, subconsciously, and consciously. It will be a very powerful experience.

Then, when you have gotten through these prompts and opened up the connection to your heart, you will be ready to dive into the deeper work.

Now... Let's get to the journaling!

JOURNAL PROMPT INSTRUCTIONS

Remember that the purpose of this journaling is primarily not about the conscious mind, your thoughts, or the words that you put down on the page - it is mainly about learning and practicing how to connect to your emotions. That's why these are 'prompts' and not 'essay assignments'. The prompts that I give you are meant to spark an emotion more than they are meant to spark a train of thought (most of them, anyway). They are meant to help you feel things that you didn't realize you felt before, and **only then** to attach some meaning to those feelings, where appropriate.

These prompts will, in fact, help point out to you - intellectually and consciously - certain blockages and limiting beliefs you have, but mostly these kinds of intellectual revelations will just happen naturally as a byproduct of connecting to your emotions. You won't 'figure out' your issues through journaling. They will be revealed to you naturally - where relevant and appropriate.

Overall, the point is to allow the writing to happen on its own. It should be a practice in automatic writing to some extent. Your goal isn't to figure out what to write and to think about it. It is to feel something, and then to get out of your way while your heart and your subconscious mind start writing on their own.

What we are doing here is training ourselves to become the listener to our own thoughts and feelings, instead of being the speaker.

In every (civil and polite) conversation, at any given moment there is a speaker and a listener. When it comes to the conversation that has been going on in our heads our whole lives, we have always seen ourselves as the speaker. You were always trying to consciously and actively think and deduce. You believed that all thought was an active and intentional process that required active effort.

We need to learn how to be the listener to our thoughts instead. How to be the passive participant in the thought-based conversation going on in our heads.

You need to start realizing that your brain is actually more like a TV than it is a computer. You receive your thoughts, you don't truly 'create' or 'deduce' them most of the time. You have no idea where your thoughts come from and there is only a small extent to which we can actually control the thoughts that we are having. 90% of the time, we are on autopilot and the thoughts are just kind of flowing through us (think about when you're trying to fall asleep and your mind just won't shut up... you're not CHOOSING to think all those things in the moment, and yet - for some reason - you still think of yourself as the speaker of your thoughts). Only in a very limited context are we actually capable of controlling our conscious thoughts.

So, our goal with these journal prompts is to allow ourselves to connect to the emotions that are actually sparking our thought cycles behind the scenes.

For each journal prompt, then, these are your instructions.

1. If possible, try and do your journaling early in the day.
2. Find yourself a quiet environment (if possible). Make sure you won't be disturbed. Turn off distractions. If you like, light incense or a candle to help create an atmosphere for reflection. Feel free to play meditation music or other calming white noise.
3. Read the journal prompt once or twice in your head to get the concept down and to let ideas start flowing. (some of our journal prompts aren't written... skip this step in that case).
4. Place your hands on your heart and close your eyes.
5. Spend 1-2 minutes like that. Focus on your breathing. Focus on your heartbeat. Focus on whatever sensations you feel in your body. Connect with how you feel in that moment, and just settle in.
6. Open your eyes, and read the journal prompt once more (skip for non-written prompts).
7. Listen and wait. Don't try to force an idea to come up. Don't try to figure out what to write. Just listen for whatever words and thoughts are popping up inside of you.
8. Even if you think that the words that come up first have nothing to do with the journal prompt you just read, as soon as something comes up, just start writing. Don't try and make sense of it. Don't try and justify it or understand it. Just start writing whatever wants to come out.
9. As you do, focus on how you feel while you're writing it.
10. Continue with this - focus on your emotions, and keep writing whatever comes to mind. **Don't question anything that comes up!** This is crucial! Whenever you find yourself analyzing or overthinking about what you're writing, bring yourself back to your inner sensations and emotions, and just keep writing whatever wants to flow through you. Focus inwards for a moment, and see if anything comes back up for you to keep writing. Remember, you are practicing getting out of your own way. Don't hesitate. Don't question. Let your subconscious

161

express itself freely. **Steps 8 and 10 are the most crucial elements of this whole process.**
11. Don't stop until you naturally run out of inspiration.
12. Set it aside and reflect on it during the day.
13. Come back to the exercise in the evening. Read what you wrote.
14. Perform the evening reflection in your head.

Remember... you are not 'searching for answers' here. Any conscious, cognitive answers about your life that you get as a result of this are more of a bonus. The REAL work here is just in doing it! The same way that meditation is not about a goal, neither is journaling. The only real goal is to give your heart and mind a safe space in which to start opening up. Every time you do a journaling exercise, whether or not you achieved any great revelation or conclusion, you DID accomplish something. You are training your brain to know that it's ok to relax and to express itself freely. This is a muscle that you are building. It is resistance that you are releasing.

Just by practicing it, you strengthen that muscle, and that's all that matters. Just by performing the act of journaling you allowed your mind to unravel a bit. Every once in a while, this provides you with a noticeable revelation or sign of growth, but most of the time it's just subtle; the same way that you don't notice your muscles getting bigger every single time you go to the gym. It is only upon reflection of where you were a month ago, compared to where you are now, that you notice any real improvement, and that is the way that you need to start understanding this entire healing process - it is a matter of building muscle.

Use this as an exercise to connect with your heart, and to get out of your own way. From there, you will allow revelations, lessons and growth to come in easily and naturally, on their own terms and in their own timing.

The important word there is 'allow'. Don't force, expect or desire any particular outcome. Simply allow whatever wants to happen, to happen. You start by applying that mentality to your journaling, because when you can learn to apply that mentality to the rest of your life... you will be free.

This is a practice. Not a mission.

Practice allowing whatever wants to happen, to happen, without getting in the way. That's all.

Good luck!

21 DAYS OF JOURNALING

Day 1 - Musical Prompt (#1)

To make sure that you fully grasp this concept that journaling is about bypassing the cognitive mind and allowing our repressed emotions to express themselves, the first prompt is not a written or a verbal prompt at all. No words. No cognition. Just emotion.

Your journal prompt for day 1 is in the form of music: Franz Shubert's famous Unfinished 8th Symphony.

Go to this link for the best version of the piece to use: https://www.youtube.com/watch?v=uWnKMzAedK4

Or just search up 'Schubert's no. 8 Unfinished Symphony'.

Once you have it loaded up and are ready to go (turn off autoplay so it doesn't go to the next video), press play and spend a few minutes just listening, eyes closed, with your hands over your heart, and when you are ready, start writing... about whatever comes into your head. You might write about emotions you are feeling in the moment, memories it brings up, what you think the piece is about, some visualization of the musical piece, or maybe some random poem or short story will spew out of you. Who knows? It doesn't matter. You are practicing not questioning whatever comes up and allowing it to flow through you. You are training your mind, body, and heart to see that it's ok to just let go.

If the piece ends before you finish writing, then continue writing in silence. Do not repeat the piece or move on to something else. If you finish writing before the piece ends, that was to be expected. It's all good.

Enjoy!

***

DAY 1 - EVENING REFLECTION:

When was the last time you truly sat down and did some deep listening like you did during this piece, where you were able to shut off from the world for a moment and focus on just what was happening? That's a rhetorical question, by the way... you don't need to think of the actual last time... merely reflect on how distracted we are in our daily lives, and what it felt like to truly just sit and listen for a moment.

Day 2 - Genie in a Bottle - Your First Wish.

Imagine that you just found a genie lamp and found out that you get three wishes. Before necessarily thinking about what your first wish will be, spend a minute or two with your hand over your heart trying to connect to the excitement and amazement you would feel in that moment. Try and truly feel as if you get to make these wishes right now; that you have been presented with this amazing opportunity to wish for anything you could ever want! Then, when you're ready, start writing out your first wish, why you want it, and how amazing your life would be when you have it (or anything else that comes to mind).

***

DAY 2 EVENING REFLECTION:

When you think about how you would feel if you got your wish, ask yourself... which do you care more about? The thing that you wished for, or the emotion you would have when you get it? If you could choose between either having that thing (but being cursed to being miserable forever) or to experience the emotion of having it for the rest of your life (but never actually attain it), which would you choose?

Recognize that your desire for the thing you wished for is an illusion, and that all you truly want is to feel good.

Day 3 - The Eyes of a Child - The First Magic:

Children see magic in everyday occurrences and sometimes they are even just convinced that something really is magic. Try to think of something that made you feel that way as a child, and try to remember the excitement and the wonder that flowed through you in that moment.

Focus on that feeling or on the thing that sparked that feeling, and when you're ready... start writing.

***

DAY 3 EVENING REFLECTION:

Was there anyone in particular or any event in particular that made you begin to feel ashamed about believing in magic or spirituality, or about just plain being a kid? What did that person or event make you feel about yourself? What beliefs do you think you developed from that experience that are holding you back today? How do you feel about that person today?

Day 4: Pure, innocent love.

Think back to one moment in your life when you experienced a truly pure and sweet moment of love. Whether it was romantic, friendly or familial doesn't matter. Maybe it was with a boyfriend or girlfriend in high school, maybe it was the one brief moment of bliss you had with the one that got away, or maybe it was a moment where a parent was just absolutely everything you needed them to be for you.

Focus on that feeling or on that moment, and when you are ready, write about that moment, how it made you feel, what you believe about love and relationships, or anything that comes to mind.

***

DAY 4 EVENING REFLECTION:

What sort of beliefs or blockages might you have built up about love and relationships over the years? Has getting hurt led you to putting up walls that are getting in the way of you truly being vulnerable again? What would it be like to get that feeling of pure love back into your life?

Day 5: One word prompt (#1)

As the title suggests - focus on the feeling of the following one-word prompt, and write whatever comes to mind:

Word of today: Beautiful

***

DAY 5 EVENING REFLECTION:

Are you willing to truly believe and accept that you are beautiful? Are you comfortable with someone telling you that you're beautiful? If not, when was the last time you felt safe receiving that kind of compliment? Who gave you the compliment, and how did it feel?

Day 6 - Your Life Right Now Prompt (#1)

Let's focus on your life right now. Think about the last time that something made you truly upset or sparked anxiety or stress. Think about that feeling. Think about what it triggered inside of you. When you're ready, start writing. Maybe you want to express how you felt in the moment and what you thought about what happened. Maybe you want to write about how you feel about the reaction you had, or maybe about the cycle of this behavior that keeps happening. Etc...

***

DAY 6 EVENING REFLECTION:

Now that you can think about this event with some form of hindsight, was the situation as big of a problem as you made it out to be at the time? Whether it was or whether it wasn't, did your reaction to it help the situation or truly feel good at all? Can you see how a lighter perspective and being more in control of your emotions could have created a better outcome? Why do you allow yourself to lose control and – more importantly – to justify your painful and self-harming emotional reactions? (I.e. why do you justify your anger and frustration instead of just learning to overcome it?)

Day 7: Conscious Reflections (#1).

Okay, this one is a little more for your conscious mind to help give you strength and reminders to fall back on when you encounter struggles on this emotional journey.

Think about some time in your life where you were facing a challenge that you never thought that you could accomplish, overcome or escape from, but by your will, strength and skills - or maybe just by luck and a little help from your friends - you managed to do what seemed impossible. How did it turn out and how did it feel?

***

DAY 7 EVENING REFLECTION:

If you made it out of and/or succeeded in that moment that you thought was impossible, why do you constantly insist that other things that you want to achieve are impossible? Why do you allow yourself to think that you're incapable of accomplishing things? Can you try to remind yourself of these unlikely past successes the next time that you're faced with a challenge?

Day 8: Musical Prompt (#2) - Opera

For today we will turn to some of the most intensely emotional music of all time, in the form of opera. The angelic peaks of the human voice are mind blowing and often instill a true sense of awe and higher awareness. Enjoy this piece, and write whatever comes to mind.

Since this piece is much shorter than the first one we used, spend a couple of minutes with your hand over your heart, focusing inwards, before you begin playing the piece:

Today's Piece: Un Bel Di Vedremo - Puccini

Search it up, or head to this link:
https://www.youtube.com/watch?v=RIXjFdkA6VU

***

DAY 8 EVENING REFLECTION:

Much like hearing the unreal, heavenly cadence of an opera singer's voice, there are things that you wouldn't believe the human body is capable of until you see it (or hear it) for yourself. Our capacity and capabilities go far beyond what we generally think, and even further than we're ready to believe. What are some ways that you think you might be holding yourself back because you have limiting beliefs about what your body is capable of?

Day 9: Genie in a bottle (#2) -

Same as the first genie exercise we did last week. After all... you get THREE wishes! The point of these exercises is to help you connect with the deepest levels of excitement that you can tap into, as well as to help you break past any limitations about what you're willing to ask for and look forward to in your life. Remember, this is a GENIE IN A BOTTLE! Think outside of the box and try to think about what would truly make you the happiest in this life, and don't be afraid to ask for it!

DO NOT HOLD BACK!

***

DAY 9 EVENING REFLECTION:

Now that I pointed out that the point of this exercise was to go all out, did you maybe notice that you went further than you did last week? Or did you maybe notice that you STILL had blockages about going all out? Don't you think it's weird that even in a fantasy exercise you won't allow yourself to ask for the VERY BEST?

Think about what that means about your inner beliefs. Think about any inner blockages you might have that are preventing you from even imagining what you want in life and how that will inevitably affect your actions and your disposition; how you will inevitably aim lower and achieve less in your life because of these limiting beliefs.

Day 10: Cherished Childhood Object -

Just about every child had some treasured object that they carried around with them everywhere. Maybe it was a blanket, a stuffed animal, a toy, etc... Think about one or all of the most treasured items you had as a child that brought you comfort and joy. Connect to that feeling, and then start writing. Feel free to write a letter to that thing thanking it for all the great times you had together. Or write about memories you have with it or just how it made you feel. Remember that feeling.

***

DAY 10 EVENING REFLECTION:

What do you think it was about that object that made you so attached to it? Most likely it wasn't an overly special object itself, and you probably held on to it so long that it was dirty and torn apart or broken by the end but you loved it intensely all the same. So, if it wasn't for its physical appearance or even its function, why be so attached to it?

Recognize that that kind of love and affection for something at that deep level is a beautiful thing that we lose when we start integrating into the 'real world' and start judging everything based on its practical value.

Love for the sake of love. That's what life should be about.

Day 11: Love at home

What did love and relationships look like in your home when you were growing up? Were your parents affectionate to each other or distant? Was your family close overall? If you had a single parent, what were their relationships like or how did them being single impact the homelife? Think about what home felt like to you in terms of love and safety and when you're ready, write about that feeling, or about what the homelife looked like, or events that happened, etc... Whatever comes to mind.

***

DAY 11 EVENING REFLECTIONS:

What positive or negative beliefs do you think might have become subconsciously programmed into you as a result of what you saw in your home? Were you trained to think that love is harmful or that it doesn't exist?

Were you trained to think that love must be earned and worked for? Or were you trained that love is to be given freely and that support, care, and safety are the norm?

How are these ingrained beliefs affecting you to this day?

Day 12: One Word Prompt (#2)

Once again, focus on the feeling of the following one word prompt, and write whatever comes to mind:

Word of today: Home

***

DAY 12 EVENING REFLECTION:

Where do you think you truly felt most 'at home' in your life? Whether it was in your actual home or at a friend or a lover's house, or even 'on stage' or 'on the road'. Where did you feel most in your element and how did it feel? If you could go back there, would you? If you can, why haven't you? I'm not saying you have to... just reflect on why you haven't.

Day 13: Your Life Right Now Prompt (#2) - Career.

Most people ended up choosing a job just because the world pushed them in that direction. Most are not doing something that fulfills them or that they truly chose. Think about how you feel about your job, and think about the circumstances in your life that led you to choose it or accept it.

If you are not currently employed, then think about your last job.

***

DAY 13 EVENING REFLECTION:

If you believe that you were forced by the world to accept this job, ask yourself if this is TRULY the case... or if some other version of you could have been more determined to make something else happen. Were you truly forced into it, or were you simply too afraid to fully be yourself and to pursue a riskier route that may have required more courage?

Don't be ashamed if you didn't follow your truest path... most people don't.

If you do love your job, then your reflection tonight should just be on gratitude that you get to do something you love for a living. You should also be double checking whether you TRULY enjoy it and find it actually fulfilling at the soul level, or if you've just limited yourself to a lesser expectation of what life could be, enough to be content in being unfulfilled. Have you just forgotten who you are?

Day 14: Conscious Reflections (#2) -

Once again, this prompt is meant to be a little more cognitive to help you realize things that will provide some conscious comfort to keep you from spiraling down during challenging times.

Do you feel like you spend more time complaining or more time appreciating what you have? Do you think that you are consciously aware and grateful of the miraculous life you get to lead just by living in the 21st century compared to the middle ages? Do you realize that people lived their whole lives just trying to physically survive one day to the next, and that you get to watch Netflix and download self-help courses even while the world is going through chaos? Do you appreciate how lucky you are, or do you compare yourself to others all the time?

***

DAY 14 EVENING REFLECTION:

Now that you understand a little more about how we are constantly training our brains, what do you think it does to you when you don't actively stop your negative, self-pitying thought cycles? You're allowing your brain to get programmed for that emotion. Don't you think that actively focusing on the positive a little more could help train your brain to be more optimistic and therefore to be more willing to do what you need to do to improve your life?

Day 15: Musical Prompt (#3) - Innuendo

This is just a masterpiece of music from my own musical hero that I think is appropriate for an exercise like this. In fact... I find it hard to believe I wrote a whole book without ever mentioning Freddie Mercury. I hope you enjoy it, and I hope it sparks some interesting thoughts and revelations.

Today's song is Innuendo by Queen. Either look it up, or head to the link below:

https://www.youtube.com/watch?v=g2N0TkfrQhY

When the song ends, just continue writing in silence until you are done.

***

DAY 15 EVENING REFLECTION:

Whether it's a musician or some other kind of performer or artist, is there anyone who fills you with a burning sense of awe, passion or inspiration whenever you see them or their work? Is there some deep part of you that gets activated when seeing something from them? Also, have you maybe left some part of your own passions around their artform behind? Is there a passion or hobby that you gave up on that maybe you don't realize how much joy you are missing out on by not doing? Is it possible for you to start pursuing some forgotten creative hobby again just for fun?

Day 16: Genie in a bottle (#3)

Your third wish! You've practiced thinking big and getting out of your own way, now let's see what you've got! Remember, the goal is to connect to the biggest and most amazing emotion of excitement and joy that you can muster. You can have any experience, achieve or have anything... do ANYTHING! Even if it defies the laws of physics and reality. What is it?

***

DAY 16 EVENING REFLECTION:

Think about the act of practicing these 'genie in a bottle' exercises and what it does for your brain. We're not just playing make believe, we're training it to feel joy and excitement. We are PRACTICING those emotions. Realize how visualizations and affirmations aren't just playtime spiritual woo-woo, they are helping us reprogram our subconscious minds which have been getting in our way our whole lives so that we can start aiming higher and taking bigger action.

Day 17: You're My Best Friend!

Who was your best friend when you were a child? What did you used to do together? Where did you used to hang out? What were some of your best memories with them? Think about all that and how it all felt, and when you are ready, write! Maybe you want to write a letter to that person as if you saw them today, or a letter to your younger self or their younger self. Maybe you just want to reminisce about good times or about how it felt. Whatever pops up.

***

DAY 17 EVENING REFLECTION:

What does friendship mean to you today compared to what it meant to you as a child? What do relationships of all kinds mean to you now compared to what they meant to you back then?

Do you think your new view of relationships and life is an improvement from what you believed as a kid, or do you feel like you lost something along the way that you'd like to get back?

Day 18: Love in Fiction

Think about a fictional (or maybe a famous) couple that - to you - was the pure embodiment of love and romance. The absolute epitome of what love could be. Think about how it felt watching them or what it would feel like to be them and when you're ready, write about love, about that couple, about the emotions it brings up to think about them or about some romantic fantasies you might have. Whatever comes up, remember to focus on the emotions and to try and get out of your own way. Just let whatever wants to come up, come up.

***

DAY 18 EVENING REFLECTION:

Compared to what you learned about love in the home, what do you think you learned about love from fiction? Was the idea of love that you got from fiction unreasonable, or do you think it's what love truly should be and that you shouldn't really settle for less than that?

Do you believe that you are worthy of that kind of love? Do you love YOURSELF enough to even allow yourself to receive that kind of love if someone was offering it to you, or would you pull away because of subconscious insecurities?

Day 19: One Word Prompt (#3) - Fear

Once again, focus on the feeling of the following one-word prompt, and write whatever comes to mind:

Word of today: Fear

***

DAY 19 EVENING REFLECTION:

Try and truly consider the depths of fear. Are you able to see how it's at the core of all of our suffering and all of our bad behavior? Can you see how jealousy, anger, and judgment are all based in fear?

They are all defense mechanisms against potential pain and discomfort either from inside ourselves or outside. If you were truly secure in yourself as a physical and spiritual being, these things wouldn't truly be an issue. The more that you can recognize that it's all about your own fear and that fear is an illusion, the more that you can learn to take control of these knee jerk emotional responses that keep you in cycles of self-harm.

Day 20: Your Life Right Now Prompt (#3) - Friendships

Think about the friends that you keep in your life. How do they make you feel? How do they treat you? Do you admire your friends? Do you hang around people who inspire you, support you, and encourage you to be better, or do they enable your bad habits because they have them too?

***

DAY 20 EVENING REFLECTION:

If your friends are exactly the friends you need them to be and are always there for you, your reflection tonight is gratitude. Don't take it for granted it. Appreciate it.

If your friends are NOT there for you or don't treat you well - if they're not respectful, if they hold you back, enable your bad habits or make you feel bad about yourself in any way - why do you think you continue to keep them as friends?

There is an obvious self-betrayal happening in toxic relationships like that, so what do you think it means about your own sense of self-worth that you allow these people into your life and continue to call them your friends?

Day 21: Conscious Reflections (#3)

How much of your life have you missed out on because you didn't know everything you learned in this book, and because you haven't truly done the deep healing yet? How have your relationships suffered? How have your hobbies and passions and inner fulfillment suffered? How has your income suffered? If you could get back in touch with who you truly were and live without fear and anxiety, and if you COULD create whatever life you wanted, what would that look like and feel like?

***

DAY 21 EVENING REFLECTION:

Is this a journey you want to go on yourself, or do you want some help? Is it worth it for you to struggle to figure out all the nitty gritty yourself and to keep missing out on life in the meantime, or... if you had a guaranteed way to speed up the journey 100 fold, would you take that help?

If you are still reading these words right now and you made it to the very end of this book, then clearly you resonate with what I have to say, you have been enjoying this process and you are ready for the next steps. Presumably, it also means that you believe what I have to say, you have seen the value I can deliver, and you believe that I have real and true wisdom to share.

If that's the case, then I highly encourage you to push past any last fears and to commit to this deeper journey with me and dive into my course. I promise, it will be the best gift you've ever given yourself... IF you put in the work and do it! I'll make it as simple and easy as possible, but you still have to put in the effort, of course.

Choose yourself. Invest in yourself. Step into your new life, asap!

http://BenjyShererCoaching.com/ffcourse

TRANSFORMATIONS I'VE SEEN

Whether you decide to work with me or not, I truly hope that these testimonials from my past clients can provide some inspiration for you about what is possible by doing this inner work. I want you to know what is possible for yourself if you commit to the inner healing, with or without me!

***

A few months ago, I had to face the truth: My life sucked... Though I tried my best to maintain a decent attitude and stoic demeanor, the reality was completely the opposite; I was suffering inside. For one reason or another, my life was not going the way I had envisioned when I was a kid. After what seemed like an endless downward spiral into a dark depression, I had no idea where to turn...

That's when Benjy appeared in my life. Skeptically, I decided to take a leap of faith...

I AM SO GLAD THAT I DID!!

Benjy gave me the tools to take full control over my life and destiny. He taught me how to connect with my inner self. He taught me how to

189

trust in my intuition and find my purpose. He taught me how happiness is a skill that can be developed and mastered. And he empowered me with the knowledge and tools to build lasting success as I move forward in my life.

In his awesome program, Benjy was with me every step of the way, from the theoretical concepts to the direct day-to-day application of techniques. These are habits that I will continue to use for the rest of my life - both in business and relationships.

Whether you need a massive transformation, or merely a friendly push to get your life on track, I wholeheartedly recommend working with Benjy.

- Daniel

I am moving into week 8 of the course and what a journey this has been. If someone would have suggested to me that just 7 short weeks ago, I would be where I am now, given the state I was in, I would have thought it to be ludicrous. I stumbled upon Benjy's webinar (I don't even remember how...it just appeared). After I watched it, I felt compelled to sign up for the free call. And I don't normally do these things. I normally sign up for them as we often do, but I don't follow through.

After the call, I had this voice telling me to take this leap and make this investment for ME... despite being financially restricted during these times. There wasn't a doubt in my mind that this was necessary. I came into this program a shattered person. I'm sure Benjy would say the same for me, but he got it. And what has transpired over these two months has been truly the best gift I have ever given to myself.

I have reclaimed myself. It's an ongoing process and this course has presented practical knowledge that is easily accessible to anyone wanting to receive it. It is without a doubt an eye opener. From an amazing coach who leads you to discover your love for yourself. The doors opening for me now are a direct reflection of my healing... and I wouldn't be here in this space now if not for this commitment. Seriously, dive in. You won't regret it.

- Laurie

My name is Michelle and please allow me to share my experience with you. This course has changed my life in a very small amount of time. I have been on a spiritual path for quite some time. I've been meditating for years and have had energy work and energy healings done. I've done soul retrievals and attended sound baths, I have taken shaman classes and done breath work. I've had attachments removed and cut energetic ties with family. I have completed all my munay ki rites and still felt lost at sea. After, I would be happy and whole but it would be gone in weeks. I recently came across Benjy's shadow work video and instantly felt something resonate. With all the work I've done, shadow work must be the piece I was missing.

On my first call with Benjy he asked me a question that stopped me in my tracks. He asked me if I loved myself. I told him of course I do! That's what this path is all about. Then he asked me to say it. The fuck! I couldn't even say it. I was lying to myself this whole time. No one had given me a starting point but now I had one. After that call I signed up. I spent the beginning of the course raising my vibration through self love and gratitude. My life started changing right there. I was finally taught the tools I needed to raise my state of consciousness. He showed me that releasing old wounds and traumas was going to get me to where I knew I was supposed to be. Getting rid of surface triggers allowed me to move forward on a more authentic path. I wasn't doing what everyone wanted me to do. I was letting go and starting my own journey.

Since releasing old habits that no longer serve me, I have made room for growth and LOVE. My relationships are deeper and more honest. I don't stress over money because the universe is always working in my favor. I know that because of this course I have manifested the beginnings of a life that is truly magical. I have a long way to go in healing core wounds but I have tools to use and a lit path to follow. All the other courses you might come across won't be as complete or as detailed as this one. Every week had specific how to's and goals to be met, with all the information on how it was technically possible. Everything he said had the evidence to support it and nothing was based on faith, although I had that too. Benjy made it feel so easy even when it got really hard. This wasn't a cake walk but I was taught how to pick myself back up and shine. Thank you for listening to my story! And thank you to Benjy, for showing me these life skills! This is the only life worth living and I have it because of his 8 week course! It's your turn.

All my best,

- Michelle

And those are just a few of my favorites!

Yours could be my next favorite! What do you think yours would sound like if I could help you achieve the same level of self love and fearlessness you just heard from others?

Find out more about my course at

http://BenjyShererCoaching.com/ffcourse

CONCLUSION AND GOODBYE

If you are reading these words right now, then presumably you read the whole book and I just want to take a moment to truly thank you from the bottom of my heart. It is truly so meaningful and so amazing that I get to share this knowledge and wisdom with you. My whole life there was this inner part of me that knew that I was here to share something with the world. I didn't know what it was or how I was going to achieve it, and I even came to believe that I was just being foolish or arrogant and that I needed to get over it.

I settled into a regular 3D life like everyone else, and although I was certainly living a unique life, living my own way and still had big dreams and hopes for my future, I had largely given up on the concept of finding true meaning or having a real impact in this life.

My awakening led me to my healing. My healing led me to my mission work (i.e. - this teaching and coaching), and the mere idea that I get to change people's lives for a living with unique wisdom that I brought with me into this Earth is mind boggling and beautiful.

Thank you for taking the time to be on this journey with me, and thank you for allowing me to be a part of your healing.

Feeling blessed, honored, and grateful,

Yours Truly,

Benjy.

WHERE ELSE CAN YOU FIND ME?

Join my FB group:
https://www.facebook.com/groups/FutureMakersUnited

Watch my webinar 'From Awakening to Ascended - completing the journey to 5D': www.BenjyShererCoaching.com/replay

Get my book *10 Mind Hacks for Quicker Emotional Healing*: I highly recommend checking this out, as it pairs very nicely with the book you just finished reading, adding a lot of practical tools to the wisdom you learned here, to help get you started and to accelerate your healing.** www.BenjyShererCoaching.com/mhbook

Find me on Youtube as 'Benjy Sherer Coaching'.

You can still find some of my earlier writings at www.TheRightSon.com

Enroll in my 8 week course:
http://BenjyShererCoaching.com/ffcourse

Don't forget to leave a review for this book on Amazon (or whatever other site you may have purchased this from).

Email me any time at BSherer@BenjyShererCoaching.com

I am available for lectures and speaking functions.

This book has been self-published. If any book agents or publishers are interested in this work, please get in touch.